M000099066

Love Yourself to Health

to Health

... with Gusto!

ABC Guide
for Surviving a
Toxic Relationship

by

JEANINE FINELLI

CCB Publishing
British Columbia, Canada

Love Yourself to Health… with Gusto!
ABC Guide for Surviving a Toxic Relationship

Copyright © 2014 by Jeanine Finelli
ISBN-13: 978-1-77143-169-9
First Edition

Library and Archives Canada Cataloguing in Publication
Finelli, Jeanine, 1971-, author
Love yourself to health… with gusto! : ABC guide for surviving a toxic relationship
/ by Jeanine Finelli. -- First edition.
Issued in print and electronic formats.
ISBN 978-1-77143-169-9 (pbk.).--ISBN 978-1-77143-170-5 (pdf)
Additional cataloguing data available from Library and Archives Canada

Jeanine Finelli may be contacted at: finellinutrition@aol.com
or through her website: www.LoveYourselftoHealth.com

Author photos by Mitch Danforth.
Other photos contained herein are the property of the author.
Cover design by Brenda Hawkes.
Edited by Phyllis Jask.

Disclaimer: SEE YOUR PHYSICIAN. The information in this book is not intended to replace that of your physician and does not constitute medical advice. Do not use this book in place of proper medical care. Readers are advised to seek professional medical assistance in the event that they are suffering from any medical problem. The statements made in this book have not been evaluated by the Food and Drug Administration. The products featured are not intended to diagnose, treat, cure or prevent any disease. All health questions concerning yourself or anyone else, must initially be addressed by your doctor or physician. The author or anyone and anything associated with the writing, production or distribution of this book assumes **ABSOLUTELY NO** liability to or for anyone who uses the information presented in this book. The reader or user of the information presented in this book assumes the entire responsibility and liability for his or her actions.

Extreme care has been taken by the author to ensure that all information presented in this book is accurate and up to date at the time of publishing. Neither the author nor the publisher can be held responsible for any errors or omissions. Additionally, neither is any liability assumed for damages resulting from the use of the information contained herein.

All rights reserved. No part of this publication may be reproduced, stored in a retrieval system or transmitted in any form or by any means, electronic, mechanical, photocopying, recording or otherwise without the express written permission of the author except in the case of brief quotations embodied in critical articles and reviews. Printed in the United States of America, the United Kingdom and Australia.

Publisher: CCB Publishing
                  British Columbia, Canada
                  www.ccbpublishing.com

To My "Second Biggest Fan"

You were there through everything. I believed in myself because you believed in me. Your friendship is priceless and I am holding this book in my hands because of you.

Praise received for
<u>Love Yourself to Health... with Gusto!</u>

"*Jeanine clearly practices what she preaches and her practical advice has such profound positive effects.*"
—Dan Thomas, Manager, Whole Foods Market®, Cary, NC

"*Jeanine gives us a book rich with encouragement that reminds us we are worthy of dignity and wellness, not only in the body, but in heart and spirit as well. Ask for help, walk barefoot in the grass, and cry when you need to—simple words of advice yet so wise, so necessary in the world of today.*"
—Gregory E. Lang, *New York Times* bestselling author of more than 20 books, including *Why a Daughter Needs a Dad*

"*Jeanine offers immense practicality, and a refreshingly lightheartedness that brings laughter and joy to the Natural Health Industry.*"
—Gabrielle R.L. Diamante, ND

"*Jeanine provides a thought-provoking and transformational guide, which shows that personal triumph trumps all suffering and that real triumph comes from within our core of confidence and from our ability to rise above our circumstances and grab on to our truth. She tells you exactly what is to come and how to push past the pain to achieve your greater purpose! This is a book that will help thousands, maybe millions, of readers to discover their True North and a path to a more divine tomorrow.*"
—Anne Bruce, bestselling author of *Discover True North*, and *Be Your Own Mentor* (McGraw-Hill)

Contents

PROLOGUE: A LOVE STORY

One chilly September morning of my New York childhood, I snuggled into a ball under the covers in my twin bed. I opened one eye to look at the clock—9:34 a.m. My younger sister had left her bed, and I had the room to myself—a rare moment in a home with four girls. The sweet smell of garlic, basil, oregano, and olive oil permeated the air. It instantly reminded me, with every breath, that it was Saturday. My mother was making a big pot of her gravy—what we New York Italians call *tomato sauce*. She would prepare it on Saturday so that Sunday morning was free to attend church at either St. Columba or St. Denis. I preferred mass at St. Columba because the cemetery at St. Denis always creeped me out.

Sundays at 3:00 always brought with it a family dinner, which as we got older included our high school boyfriends. In a home filled with daughters, I think my mom delighted in cooking for hungry, strapping teenage boys almost as much as those boys loved eating her perfectly prepared Italian dinners. As the typical Italian dinner would have it, there were at least three loud, simultaneous conversations going on, a bread basket being passed back and forth, lots of laughter, and Italian music in the background. The album my mother usually chose was called *Italian Gold*. My father would begin with a toast that included how cool God is and how lucky he is to have his wife and family.

My parents met at just 16 years old. My dad joined the Marines at 18 years old and went to Camp Lejeune in North Carolina for basic training. On weekends while all of his friends were gearing up for strip clubs, women, and drinking, my father was catching a ride with another Marine to the Bronx or even hitchhiking home just to see my mother, his then 19-year-old girlfriend. His mother was always so excited to see him, too. Hitchhiking every weekend form North Carolina to New York to see your girlfriend? Who does that anymore? Even then, his dedication to my mother was unsurpassed.

After eating a very filling dinner, my father would always do the dishes because my mother cooked, and it wasn't unusual for him to put on different music to accompany the task. It could be anything from Jerry Vale, to Pink Floyd, to Harry Nilsson. The possibilities were endless—and endless possibility was such a lesson my dad taught us.

As I crept out of bed that chilly September morning, I heard music playing in the living room of our split-level home. I opened the door and walked toward the stairs only to see all three of my sisters sitting on the avocado-green carpeted steps that led to the spot where the front hallway, kitchen, and living room met. At the bottom of the steps rested our regal German shepherd Hope. It seemed that she also basked in the loving energy that filled our home.

What I witnessed that day is etched in my memory forever. My parents were lovingly dancing to "I Only Have Eyes for You" by the 50s group The Flamingos. The sunlight streamed in through the living room and made it even more of a divine moment. My parents had no idea we were perched there like four little mourning doves—at least at first they didn't. After all, their love and dedication for their marriage was no secret in our home. Sure, they disagreed and even got upset with one other at times, but those times were rare, and when it did happen, we saw their relationship "dance" gently to bring them back into a place of peace and love. Only during those times of stress, the dance steps were forgiveness, patience, and trust.

Even today, they still hold hands, kiss, and actually deeply enjoy each other's company. We were raised to believe that true love is kind, respectful, playful, loyal, and that kindness is also choice. You can choose to do what creates union in your relationship or you can choose to act on things that create separation and division, like paying more attention to the person you are texting than to the living, breathing person who is sitting right in front of you. How might that morning on the stairs watching my parents dance have changed if my dad's cell phone rang? What if my mom's phone chirped with a Facebook message from an old boyfriend who commented on her photo and told her how lovely she still looked?

♣♣♣

The romance novel of my life has played out a quite differently. Looking back, it all makes sense to me now, but for a long time I danced my own dance—one of unhappiness and discontent. I am so grateful for my path, and finally I have found peace within. Most importantly I learned a valuable lesson from all of my good and not-so-good decisions. And for that reason, I always come back to realize that I really am no different than my parents. It does indeed take two to tango. Stepping on your partner's foot is to be expected once in a while; it happens, and it's normal. But when you are dancing the waltz, and your partner is dancing the jive, there is no rhythm, no flow, no common goal, and sadly, no joy. It is because of my parents that I have finally found the love of my life...me! Of course, my kids are the light that keeps my heart beating, but how can we love anyone fully if we do not love and respect ourselves?

My vigilant pursuit of traditions, centeredness, simplicity, and love have all come from what I so naturally bore witness to daily in my formative years before I married and moved from New York to North Carolina at the age of 21. It is all with me, every bit of it, and it is my duty and, I feel, God's will that as a human being, a woman, and a mother, I provide my children with the healthiest landscape that I can, no matter what adversities arise. I wish for them to love themselves and nurture their souls in a world that is relentless with its focus on constant distractions, image, labels, and appearances.

xi

Mom and Dad at 23 years old with two children.
The most gorgeous couple I know.

ACKNOWLEDGMENTS

Thank you, Mom and Dad for walking the talk. You protected and valued our family traditions, and you always set an example that love is kind. It is because of your choices and God's guidance that I have been able to be strong enough to get through the challenges and devastation that have gripped hold of my very core. I still believe in the fairytale because I lived it. I was in it. You made me your princess.

I am thankful to my true friends who never left my side, ever, and to Anne Bruce for reminding me to follow my True North.

I am especially grateful for my dearest children Domenic and Lily. I would do it all again to be your mother—even if it was just for a single day and just for one hug. I am humbled, honored, and entirely fulfilled by your love. I gave you life, but through you, I learned how to live it.

I give countless thanks to my friend and colleague Dr. Tatiana Irvin (www.nurturing-hands.com). You helped me to release the past and embrace my future. You are brilliant and I thank you for lighting my inner candle, encouraging me to know my truth, and helping me to be at peace with what I found.

I thank my dear friend Bonnie, without whom, thousands, including me, would be forever lost.

I am infinitely grateful for Divine Guidance for all of the ways in which my heavenly support showed up to guide me in my darkest and my brightest moments.

I thank my Love. I had no idea that loving myself to health would lead me to you. You surprise me at every turn, and the coolest thing is you aren't even trying to. I am the luckiest girl.

And last, I thank all of the people who decided to turn a blind eye to the truth and stick their heads in the sand. Sometimes life calls for rising to occasions we would rather not, but as adults we must do what children cannot. I never knew I was capable of being so strong.

ABOUT THE AUTHOR

Jeanine Finelli is a Certified Health Coach and Speaker with a private counseling practice who agrees wholeheartedly that life can be hectic and believes in healing from the inside out. After a life-threatening auto accident at age sixteen, a career in travel, and years of work in the pharmaceutical industry, Jeanine felt a deep calling to play a larger role in the disease prevention and health wellness of others. She inspires her clients to create a life that supports healing and is committed to her role and influence as a mother.

Jeanine earned her Health Coach Certification from the Institute of Integrative Nutrition® in NYC in 2008, and has learned from Dr. Mehmet Oz, Dr. Andrew Weil, David Wolfe, Joshua Rosenthal, Walter Willett, and many more.

She is the host of Love Yourself to Health blog talk radio and works alongside skilled executive wellness physicians in Cary, NC. She conducts private phone sessions for clients nationwide, and believes in practicing what she preaches. Jeanine's two children are all the reason she needs to leave a legacy of wellness behind her.

To learn more about what Jeanine does, visit:

www.jeaninefinelli.com

INTRODUCTION

I'm here to tell you that you don't have to be a prisoner in an unhealthy, dysfunctional relationship. You can be a survivor—one who lives a life with gusto! What is gusto? It's choosing to live with zest and delight. It's playing barefoot in the warm summer rain, having a full-fat cappuccino when you can have the "skinny," it's singing because it feels good, and it's choosing to be as healthy as possible despite your roadblocks. Gusto is they joyous way in which you love your body, mind, and soul like only you can.

Picking up the pieces of a broken life doesn't mean you have to lose your physical and mental health in the process. Just the opposite in fact—you can come out of a toxic relationship healthier than you ever were before. This book is a resource for you for when you're feeling small, vulnerable, and powerless. The advice I give is not intended to replace the advice given by your physician, but it can be your companion as you trudge down your own path. Because of my own journey and the trek I made from zero to hero, I wanted to write this book so that each and every human being who feels alone will know that they are far from it. Not only that, but I felt called to share with you the ways in which I fortified myself when it seemed the odds were greater of my winning the lotto than coming through a debilitating relationship more whole and even healthier than when I went in.

I've always felt a deep and visceral calling to know myself and to ignite the passion in others to come to know themselves as well. When I graduated from The Institute of Integrative Nutrition® in NYC in 2008, I decided to focus my health coaching practice around a whole-person approach. I wanted to teach my clients to connect food cravings to the current goings-on and stressors in their lives, like a demanding boss or PMS.

This approach would show them how daily stress in their relationships could disturb their sleep hormones just as much as the steady stream of caffeine that they were having throughout the day.

This whole-person approach places control back where it belongs—in your hands! Getting healthy can ultimately become the greatest detox of your life—one that is all-encompassing and spans from reducing sugar in your diet and using natural products on your body all the way to managing negative coworkers and unhealthy personal relationships.

I am six years into my health coaching business, and even though this book is geared toward the women who make up most of my practice, men can benefit from the wisdom within as well. I have been humbled that I am able to guide a multitude of beautiful feminine souls—male ones, too!—through the healing process as it relates to food, lifestyle, stress, and relationships.

It is my hope for you that these ABCs of building better health will leave you healthier, happier, whole, and maybe even a little hotter as you heal and strengthen. This book is a reminder that you are never, ever alone. Not only are you not alone, but that dignity is your God-given right, and that dignity is there even when a mean spirit is trying to rob you of it. You will learn about foods, supplements, and lifestyle tips that will fill you up because, Bella my friend, it's time for you to heal. Each and every one of my entries in this book has had a unique and irreplaceable influence on my healing and in how I built a more robust self. Some topics may apply more to your situation than others, but hopefully all will get you thinking.

RECOGNIZING DESTRUCTIVE RELATIONSHIPS

I find it fascinating that for some people, the quest for wellness can begin with the simplest of shifts, such as a routine exercise program or adding more dark leafy greens to their diet. As the years go by, the same people who have made a small shift are now exercising almost daily, making gorgeous green smoothies at home, and have finally said *no* to a relationship that has them feeling broken.

The bottom line is that destructive relationships rob you of every security that you want to feel. They intimidate and suffocate you and have you believing, on some sick level, that this is what you deserve. Every human being has the ability to be difficult or destructive at times; after all, nobody's perfect. I think that all of us have the capacity to wound another soul. A quote that comes to mind is, "People who live in glass houses shouldn't throw stones." Boy, it sure seems there are plenty of people out there who so quickly forget that they aren't perfect, yet they are willing to downright condemn others.

Saying something intentionally hurtful to your partner you wish you hadn't is surely something everyone can relate to. However, I think the difference between difficult and destructive lies in the after moments. The destructive person will never feel remorse or guilt for saying words that hurt. If they happen to apologize, it will never be in a love language that speaks to you. Why? Because they tend to apologize to make themselves feel better, not you. Or they do it to create the illusion of an empathy that they really don't possess.

The terms **narcissistic** and *sociopathic* surely come to mind here. These types of people will always portray one image, yet under their façade, they personify lies and a completely altered personality with an agenda—and that agenda doesn't include less strife and more kindness in their relationship with you! Destructive personalities exhibit ongoing displays of one or more of the following characteristics: emotional abuse, verbal abuse, physical abuse, neglect, and financial control. They demonstrate a pattern of abuse through hiding, misleading, pretending, neglecting, and telling untruths all while they weave a web of confusion around you. Before long, they are telling you that you are the reason things are spiraling downward and that if you would change, things would improve! It's a well thought out game to many of them; after a while, you actually begin to believe that you can change the situation. Wrong!

I think these people are like the Dementors from J.K. Rowling's *Harry Potter*. They live to suck every ounce of good out of you in order to make themselves feel bigger and better than you. They further divert any negative attention away from themselves in order to get the focus primarily on your so-called shortcomings. They desperately need you to believe their lies, lest the façade of their world comes crumbling down. The blocks of this façade are image, child number one, child number two, friends, family, work, type of home, type of car, type of shoes, type of exercise, and on and on. This is all so harsh, but the reality is that if your relationship is destructive and is repeatedly sabotaging your health, emotions, and your well-being, then it isn't kind—and it sure as hell isn't love.

It seems to me—and I'm neither a psychiatrist nor a psychologist—that there are too many reasons as to why someone would be so incredibly toxic to another human being. Because I work with hundreds of women, I have seen many different situations that ultimately come down to this: stay and die or leave and live.

I have met women who are reeling from finding out their husband has another wife and child elsewhere. Can you imagine the tension when he came "home"? Can you picture what a blow to the wife's self-worth that would be? Can you imagine the feeling of living a lie and every time something ceased making sense to you, you overlooked it because you have children whom you adore?

I have met other women who are married to men who are non-straight. I say non-straight because *gay* implies that these men are living or wanting to live an entirely homosexual lifestyle, which isn't always the case. Many of these non-straight men will have gay sex in addition to sex with their wives in order to convince themselves they aren't gay. To many of these men in the closet, gay is a lifestyle: It's falling in love with a man, buying a home, and adopting a baby. Another such group of men will never associate with being gay because all they want is 10 minutes of gay sex before leaving the office, but they want to come home to a wife and children and snuggle on the couch and watch a chick flick. Others come home from the gay sex soiree, and self-loathe so much that upon coming home, they are angry, mean, controlling, and bound and determined to find fault with their wife.

Let me be clear here that I am not passing any judgment on any sexual preference or lifestyle, and I am not pigeonholing all people into one of the above categories because there are as many scopes and situations as there are people. In the situation above, he is feeling so shameful that he must find something wrong with you! Without even knowing it, you were dragged into the closet.

I have met yet other women whose destructive relationships include, but aren't limited to, continued betrayal in heterosexual situations or being in a relationship with someone with an undiagnosed and untreated bipolar personality. In these situations, it seems that the pendulum is always swinging from one side to the other generally with little warning. An event that elates a bipolar person one day can trigger rage the next. The behavior is unpredictable and can be very scary because there is nothing you can do to prevent it, and there are no warnings. The ripple effects filter throughout the home and can send children scurrying to their room to get away from yet another episode that leaves plenty of whats, whys, and hows that will never be answered. The radical behavior will never make sense to them. How could it? It doesn't make sense to you, and you're a grown-up!

Whatever the toxic situation you're facing, the triggers are endless and usually ridiculous. The blueberries you bought aren't the size they like, you asked for sex because it had been weeks or years, or you asked what time they were coming home for dinner. In the case of closeted behavior, these men hate you because you are a female, they feel trapped, and you are nothing more to them than a cover and the warden to their prison. You look like a girl, smell like a girl, laugh like a girl, want love and intimacy like a girl, and it is driving them crazy. How dare you have needs, you selfish woman!

This type of neglect year after year is a slow death of your femininity and all the things that you embrace about feeling alive and being a woman. You're constantly hearing things like if you were nicer, neater, prettier, kinder, cooler, more athletic, blah blah blah, then they would want to be around you. So you try to change everything you can about yourself inside and out: clothes, hair, attitude, everything. You try not to ask questions, you try to trust, you suppress every need and desire you have. Suppress, forget, and move on becomes your survival motto. And that sweet, feminine, loving part of you dies so that you can just survive while you're feeling worthless.

I've seen women who are in relationships where there is depression, drug use, and familial issues that stem way back into their partner's childhood. One universal characteristic of these angry people is a lack of connection to self, and thus a lack of connection to Source or God. Time and time again, these abusers fill their spiritual void with all things here and now—material things, physical pleasure, instant gratification—and damn the consequences. They don't recognize the enormous black hole that exists within them because their self-worth may be wrapped up in more of what others (except you, of course) think and less of what God may want for them.

Is it fair that they make you their target? No, but you were never promised a fair life. Just look at the living conditions that other humans have to struggle with daily, and yet somehow, they have the greatest and strongest faith of anyone, anywhere, of anytime.

Although I refer to wife and husband in the previous section, the two roles I speak of are interchangeable. It is not always the man who is in the closet—sometimes it's the woman. It's not always the man who has a mental illness and it's not always the woman who is the one trying to salvage some shred of the relationship. It goes both ways. I also want to be clear that not all people "in the closet" sexually are angry or abusive. I'm neither a man hater, a Valentine's Day hater, or a wedding hater, nor am I here to place my mere judgment on anyone else's choice of how to live.

GETTING BACK YOUR POWER

Only you will be able to determine where the crack or canyon lies in your relationship. Only you will know when you have had enough and when you are ready to recognize the loop that keeps replaying in your thoughts. Then you can decide if you want to hit rewind and replay it another ten thousand times. Stillness speaks, and when you listen to that little voice inside of you that tells you that you aren't crazy, and that you know there is more to it than this, I urge you, never let that voice of God go—especially during those times you are told you are a lunatic, jealous, crazy, stupid, or anything else negative. Just when you are beginning to recognize what is really happening, they try to get you off track. That's how they do it—and it works, doesn't it?

Do you continually question yourself and the facts? Is your behavior allowing him to control you because he always has been able to (and he knows it)? Like Eleanor Roosevelt said, "No one can make you feel inferior without your consent." Your consent is not "please abuse me more"; your consent, rather, is the way you react to his bullying and intimidation. You react by accepting it, staying, keeping calm, and carrying on as if the abuse never happened. He knows your triggers and your breaking points all too well.

The message I want you to take away from this book is that you are hereby validated to begin to leave your death trap. When something is no longer causing your soul to grow, expand, and connect to its truth, you will get dragged into a black hole if you don't find a path out. A path that is authentic. A path that nurtures your body, your mind, and your soul. A path that is your choice to walk because you want to. It is never about prettier, smarter, neater, or thinner. It is about your toxic partner's black hole that sucks everything in its path—including you—into the abyss.

Once you become soul sick, heart sick, and physically sick, the choice is yours. Do you want more of the same, or do you want to live? Every hurtful word, every physical blow, every unloving gesture, every moment of deceit, every feeling of betrayal is brewing inside you. Those things seep into your core and destruct the pillars of your health. The results are low self-esteem, loneliness, acting out sexually or withdrawing sexually, fear, failure syndrome, and unresolved resentment. Those effects then manifest into physical effects such as addictions (alcohol, prescription drugs, caffeine, sugar, smoking), allergies from depressed immune function, insomnia, high blood pressure, eating disorders, panic attacks, phobias, rashes, migraines, digestive issues such as heartburn, and weight gain or weight loss. Unless you roll up your sleeves and love yourself to health, no one can do it for you.

Worse yet, do you want to bring any of those conditions to your next relationship? I'm not necessarily talking about a romantic relationship. Your relationships with your children, friends, parents, and coworkers require you to be present, use fear to your advantage, and live authentically if you want those dealings to be benevolent for all involved.

As a Certified Health Coach and mother of two, I cannot stress enough how imperative it is that you learn to weather the storm and destruction that a negative relationship will, if not immediately, ultimately have on your body, mind, spirit, weight, cravings, sleep, energy level, and even your mood. Self-preservation may not be as tangible as the flood insurance that you can purchase along with other emergency supplies should you face a weather-related disaster. Yet, make no mistake about it, the constant onslaught of emotional devastation will tear you down and erode your physical and emotional well-being.

I'm here to tell you that you can experience betrayal, deceit, control, and emotional abuse without sabotaging your well-being. This I promise you. While others may deem you worthless, remember that you are priceless. Sometimes you can go inward and protect yourself from the abuse, but many times, you just don't have the strength to and you feel like dying. That's because your gut is telling you that you *are* dying a slow death. First you die emotionally, then spiritually, then physically.

You want desperately to build up an iron-clad layer of protection so that someday the betrayal doesn't hurt. What tends to happen, though, is that by dulling your senses to toxicity, you tend to deaden your senses to joy because vulnerability is the only path to both. Even after you wake up, get dressed, and drop the kids at school then sit in meetings at work, the damage is still smoldering inside you. It's like hammering nails into a fence then taking the nails out and thinking the holes left behind will magically disappear.

I want you to realize that a chronic situation that tears you down is creating a perfect arena for illness to thrive because mental, physical, and emotional illnesses are all exacerbated by the forces of stress. Add to that nutritional slaughter, and your health really begins to erode.

FINDING YOUR HOPE

The silver lining is that you can roll up your sleeves, get support, develop a plan, and free yourself from guilt. You must walk one fearful step at a time toward freedom. There is only one way out, and it is through the pain. On the other side of that pain awaits a blanket of grace, serenity, and love just waiting to wrap you up and hold you close. If you honor your ticker as the most valuable thing you own, no one can break it or take it. In divorce and separation, there is so much focus on negotiations such as who gets the leather sofa, or the flat screen TV, or time with the children. Remember this: your health is not up for grabs like a piece of art. Take it off the table right now because it is completely non-negotiable. Honor, feed, and nurture it well. When your heart pounds in your chest with worry, fear, anxiety, and sadness, it is begging for you to love it in return as much as it has loved you. After all, if it is still beating, then it's not broken. And that, Bella, is a score!

Cultivate yourself like the little pebble of grainy sand that gets trapped inside the oyster shell only to someday yield a perfectly imperfect pearl. This book is my gift to you. I once heard someone say, "You cannot have peace until you have all of the pieces." It's true. Create a vibrant, healthy you and future for yourself. At the end of the day, what advice would you give your daughter or someone you love? Stay and die, or leave and live? What better way to show her how to honor herself, and should she ever find herself in the company of a Dementor, she will recognize it for what it is and know that with self-love, all things are possible. Love is kind and it starts with loving yourself!

If at any moment in time you feel that your safety or well-being is in danger, or the well-being of those you love, please contact the appropriate support—be it 911, your family members, or legal counsel. Your safety should always be number one priority!

A

On your journey to self-health, it's best to start at the beginning, just like Glinda, the Good Witch in *The Wizard of Oz*, told a lost and forlorn Dorothy. So many wonderful things begin with *A;* these are just a few of my favorites. Each item offers its own healthy benefit. Start slowly and try to incorporate one thing at a time so you can begin to build new, healthy habits that will stick with you for a lifetime.

ALOE VERA

No doubt what comes to mind is the spiky plant with the gooey middle that moms and grandmas used for skin care and burn relief. Did you know that aloe is just as healing for your inside as it is for your outside? It is truly a miraculous plant, and it's considered a top-10 superfood because it's off the charts with nutrients and antioxidants. Externally, it aids with things like psoriasis, scar removal, cooling and soothing burns, and clearing blemishes. Internally, it aids digestion, kills yeast, reduces certain inflammation of the gut, helps to absorb B12 and other nutrients, and helps to combat acid reflux. Wow, I just described symptoms that millions battle with daily! You can use it on any part of the body; it's one of the best anti-aging weapons you will ever own. (Don't even get me started on the cost of "anti-aging" products in department stores. Nonsense!) I have noticed my laugh and cry lines soften after continued dabs of aloe vera around my eyes. Stay fit inside and out with raw, unprocessed, and unheated aloe vera. Be mindful because aloe contains aloin, which is a substance that can foster loose bowel movements. Maybe you would even welcome an extra trip to the bathroom! After all, those bumper stickers that read

HAPPINESS IS A GOLDEN RETRIEVER are wrong. My clients feel that HAPPINESS IS A GOOD POOP!

Even the aloin-free brands support the body's detoxification and elimination process. I like Country Life®, Herbal Aloe Force®, and Lakewood®. Never ingest the aloe from your house plant unless it is potted in organic soil—unless you like eating herbicides, pesticides, and other toxic chemicals. Whichever aloe you purchase, a little goes a long way, and you'll get what you pay for. Aloe gel is thicker than aloe juice and can be somewhat gross to swallow, which is why most people prefer the juice. When buying, look for low-temperature processed or raw because heat kills its vital nutrients. You can dilute it with water, add it to a smoothie, or just knock it back from a shot glass! Don't confuse the many aloe drinks and ready-made beverages on the market today with the straight up aloe vera juice or gel. Skip those—they're packed with added sugar and most use low-quality aloe vera; read the label if you are unsure about the ingredients.

Pucker up today and enjoy my very own liver-loving Aloe-Tini. It's time to begin healing from the inside out.

Aloe-Tini

- 3 ounces aloe juice
- 2 ounces *unsweetened* cranberry juice
- Splash of seltzer
- Squeeze of fresh lime

Fill a cocktail shaker with ice, then add all ingredients. Give it a good shake and serve in your favorite martini glass. *Salud*!

ALONE TIME

The older I get and the more depth and breadth that my soul experiences, I find that my inner GPS points me toward moments when I can be with just myself. Once I have arrived at destination Jeanine, my true thoughts and feelings can safely peek out and bring clarity to my brain without distraction from others. The self-rejuvenation that comes with that experience is priceless. I love the opportunity to spend time with family and friends; however, just as much as I adore those fulfilling moments, I find it essential to create time alone to nourish myself.

So, what does that look like for me? Waking up early before the kids do and sitting on my deck watching the mourning doves that are unsuspectingly being watched by me. Or maybe it's a bath filled with Epsom salt and essential oils. It may even mean being whisked away into the story line of a riveting book that has the power to temporarily take me away. One of my all-time favorites is when I put on my daughter's pink zebra-striped headphones and plug them into my iPhone. There, but for a few moments, I am back in Tuscany or dancing in a club in New York with my girlfriends. Sometimes I even start belting out a few verses, and I bring entirely new meaning to the phrase *joyful noise*.

When was the last time you connected to yourself? It's okay, Bella...the world will not stop if you step out for a moment onto a less congested path. Allow the noise from others to go away and resist your compulsion to feel guilty. In fact, this time alone is crucial to your survival, and it's nonsense if any person tells you otherwise, ever. Whether it's morning coffee alone, a walk, or just an extra long shower, make the time for yourself. It's vital to your well-being.

APPLES

Apples are practically the perfect food. They travel well, satisfy your need to chew, are crunchy, don't require refrigeration, come in many varieties, pack more than five grams of fiber, contain pectin (which is great for digestion), and satisfy a sweet tooth! Always choose organic because they taste a million times better than conventional. Try it for yourself if you are a non-believer. Apples are one of the few foods that my kids immediately taste the difference in organic versus conventional. How could something that has been sprayed with herbicides, fungicides, and pesticides from when it was just a baby bud on a tree taste like nature intended? Do you really think you can peel away the chemicals? Knowing that conventionally grown fruit is doused with toxic chemicals at every growth stage, I can safely assume it is about as pure as the apple Snow White ate. Give your digestive tract a treat today with a nice, juicy organic apple and take a little tiny baby step in the fortification of *you.*

AROMATHERAPY

I've heard that the sense of smell is the sense that is most connected to memories. That must be why the aroma of garlic and olive oil takes me back to being a kid growing up in an Italian family. For me, that smell evokes comfort, safety, and love. Likewise, catching a whiff of Drakkar Noir and Polo cologne can transport me right back to my high school days and the boys from my youth! Smelling something can evoke a memory, but so does remembering a smell! There are two very distinct times in my life when I felt as if I were stepping into a real life Yankee candle. The first was on a family trip to San Francisco when we squeezed in a day trip to Muir Woods. I can remember the clear, crisp, cool depth of that scent in that forest. The second time was when my son and I went zip lining in the misty mountains of Costa Rica. That feeling of whizzing over distant waterfalls, hearing nothing except the sound of the wind passing my cheeks and my glove on the line wire, and zipping in and out of the mist lives deep within me. The smell of the Costa Rican air enveloping me made me want to breathe it all in forever. I wanted to transport every last sniff home with me and save it for a rainy day.

Somehow, I did. I use these memories and scents for days when I feel like my spirit is being challenged or sabotaged by toxic people. Scent is my secret weapon, a bubble I can go inside when life's relentless challenges come banging on my door. My daily aromatherapy includes candles (soy or beeswax), and I enjoy various essential oils that I incorporate into my living space.

I encourage you to do some research of your own. What smells take you back with just one whiff? Which one sets you free in the moment? Aromatherapy can help you return to your peaceful place when your relationship is anything but. Never underestimate the power that fragrance has on the mind. Inhale and exhale your way to a blissful moment where no toxicity can thrive. In that moment—in that one breath—is clear and crisp air wrapped around positive thoughts and memory that guard your happiness and emotional wholeness.

ASK

Many of us have been conditioned, as a result of our chronic adversity, to be so independent and self-sufficient that it terrifies us to ask for help. People can't read our minds; when we expect them to and they fail, bad things and hurt feelings can happen. It is vital that you communicate your needs and fears to those you can trust. Sometimes the smallest things become monumental acts of kindness, and love is kind. Remember, you are in survival mode and by asking for a helping hand when you need it most, you're keeping yourself in the eye of the hurricane and protecting yourself from being swept away by Category 5 winds. I thank God for friends and family who were always there to support me as I weathered my own relationship storm. I see many self-sufficient women who feel guilty asking for help. Why do that to yourself? I hereby give you a free pass to ask for what you need today. You don't win any awards for going it alone or for feeling over-scheduled and out of control. Learn to ask for help.

Below are a few things that I have asked for over the years. They may seem insignificant, but at the time, they were the difference between sanity and throwing my hands up in the air.

- Can you pick up my son from carpool today?
- Can I use your dryer? Mine is broken.
- How much will this cost me in a year?
- Can I borrow coffee creamer? I'm all out!
- Can you proof this email for me?
- I'm interested in that job; can you find out more about it for me?
- She is sick and asleep. Can you swing by CVS® and get Motrin®?
- Are you awake? (text at 4:00 a.m.—and my friend would reply)
- Dear Lord, Please show me the way.

Sometimes the answer will be no, but your good friends won't tell you you've lost your mind for asking something crazy, and they will still be there tomorrow. Chronic survival mode tends to keep us armed and ready, and the reality is that when your relationship is slowly killing your soul, you can indeed lose your mind. Sometimes it's as if the grimness of your situation would swallow you whole if it could; so ask for help, and don't lose your sanity here—not for this. You may have to dig pretty deep some days to find a ray of light, and some days you've just got to put out there what you need.

Look at your calendar for the week. Are there any crunch days where you could use a little help from your friends? They'll never know you unless you ask.

ATTORNEY

If the word *attorney* makes you cringe, you are not alone. Many women—me included—feel the same way. You know you need one, but how do you begin to find someone that doesn't fit the typical lawyer profile of "likes to create strife to in order to just keep billing you." When I first started searching for a lawyer I was apprehensive, so I decided to screen several lawyers in my city. Obviously if you are in a big city, you have more options to choose from than someone who lives in a small town; that doesn't necessarily mean there are no good lawyers in your area. Ask trusted friends and do research online. Most lawyers charge for a consultation, which can run anywhere from $100 to $800 depending on where you live.

Choosing your attorney is kind of like buying a pair of jeans: you need to shop around to find your best fit. You may feel at the end of the initial consultation that this attorney doesn't really care about you or your family; sadly, you may be right. After several consultations with different attorneys, I left feeling disheartened and uneasy. One female lawyer typed notes into her laptop and avoided eye contact with me as I shared my most intimate concerns and fears. I felt she was entirely disconnected from my situation. One male lawyer had vastly different beliefs than I did about what was acceptable behavior and what was not. Do lawyers have a code of ethics to follow? I believe they do. Do different lawyers feel excitement and challenge over different types of cases? Yes, of course. Does the truth sometimes get twisted or manipulated? Sure it does. Choosing a lawyer who you are comfortable with and can best represent you during an emotional divorce process is an important step in taking back your life.

After booking and paying for various consults in my community, I found my lawyer. She was attentive, looked me in the eyes, listened, asked questions, was calming and solid, and was every bit a woman just as much as she was my legal counsel. I finally felt that I was a human being with a story to be heard and not just a payment toward someone's summer trip through Europe. Legal guidance is a huge financial undertaking and is often the reason why people stay married or settle for far less than they deserve. It is a scary process no doubt, but a good attorney can make it somewhat less so.

My advice is to ask your lawyer what his/her projected cost is and stay on top of your monthly invoices so you know exactly how much that email or phone call to him/her will cost you. Good representation is a must if you are seeking justice for what is right regarding your children and finances. Remember to keep your eye on the prize: A life filled with harmony and gratification.

AVOCADOS

During the "fat makes you fat" era in the 1980 and 1990s, avocados got such a bad rap! They are actually very healthful and rich in fiber, protein, folic acid, and many other vitamins. Avocados are the fruit from a tall evergreen-type tree that can grow up to 65 feet tall. Healthy fat is a necessary macronutrient in every diet, and avocados are just that. One small avocado can contain upwards of 15 grams of monounsaturated and polyunsaturated fat, and minimal amounts of saturated fat.

While we are on the topic of fat, saturated fats in small doses are necessary, especially in their natural form like avocados and coconuts. These types of saturated fats can actually help the body lower cholesterol. If there is one fat to fear, it is transfat. This is the processed fat that clogs arteries and causes a multitude of health issues: the molecules bind together to create blockages in your body over time. Transfats are listed in the ingredients as *partially hydrogenated oil*, and slowly are being banned.

Avocados are fantastic in omelets, as guacamole, or in salads, and are a great substitute for mayo. Because they have protein, fiber, and fat, they are fantastic filler-uppers. The harder ones usually need two or three days on your countertop to ripen. Life has many fears, but avocados shouldn't be among them.

B

B is not just a letter, it's a great verb. Be true to yourself. Be authentic. Be happy. Just Be. These *B*s and the others I've listed here are fantastic for nourishing your broken heart and spirit.

BAKE

When I was about 10, Santa Claus brought me an Easy Bake oven. It became a tool for me to create tiny, scrumptious cakes that I would frost and decorate for my sisters and parents. Fast forward to my adulthood, and I still love to bake for my kids and loved ones. For me, it's the process of baking, more so than eating the actual treat, that is really the soul food. It is the smells, the creation, the family time, the anticipation, the celebration of holidays, the memories, and the sitting down snuggled together with my kids savoring every bite that brings me bliss. I find it undeniably fulfilling listening to Frank Sinatra croon *Have Yourself a Merry Little Christmas* while the tree lights are on, the crisp air outside smells like snow, and I'm baking an Italian favorite called s*truffoli* (Google *Yankee magazine baked struffoli* and fall in love!). Although each season brings with it something unique, autumn rocks it for me with crunchy leaves, open windows, and a home filled with the smell of baking pumpkin bread. Sometimes I add a few (ok, lots!) of chocolate chips to the recipe. The smell of baking goods just makes me happy.

Here's a few key baking tips: replace oil in recipe with plain applesauce and 1 tablespoon oil; experiment with half sugar and half stevia; add ¼ less sugar than what the recipe calls for;

use whole grain flour instead of white; experiment with gluten-free cakes—and enjoy!

Baking is a way for me to nurture my creative juices while someone is trying to pull the plug on my juicer of life. Was there ever a time when you enjoyed baking? Maybe it's time to dust off the old family recipes or even try something new. Own your kitchen and bake a treat for yourself or the whole family. What sounds good to you? What smells good? When was the last time you savored it? Behold the joy of creation, and allow you to be you.

BARE FEET

I feel like a lot of women have a love of boots, but I cringe when I see them. Yes, they look nice, but I *hate* having my feet trapped! I love flip flops and sandals, and the feel of sun on my toes. I have even been known to wear toe socks (I like those on www.gaiam.com) with flip flops in the fall and winter. I love to walk barefoot whenever possible and feel the crunchy leaves or soft grass under my feet. There is something so therapeutic about connecting to nature because all of our surroundings these days are so synthetic. Floors, offices, schools, carpets, shoes, and malls are all artificial surfaces that keep us disconnected from nature. Because we can't always sit on the beach or have picnics in the grass during our lunch hour, we must create time to connect to Mother Nature. The next time you can, take off your shoes and become grounded with nature, and *feel* the Earth below you. You must root to rise, Bella—root to rise.

BATH

I know you are thinking, *Good one, Jeanine!* Between phone calls, homework, soccer carpool, meetings, preparing lunches for the next day, or just wanting to sit down and enjoy a glass of wine or tea, where is there time for such frivolousness as a bubble bath? Think again! The Romans were right about this, too. A shower has a place in society for sure, even though it's a relatively new invention thought to be about 150 to 200 years old: it is fast, refreshing, hygienic, and easy to grab at home or the gym. Baths, on the other hand, require more time and undoubtedly make you feel guilty—guilty because you are filling up a big tub with all that water, guilty because now there will be 30 minutes where you are completely unapproachable by your kids who may need you to tuck them in...*again*, guilty because you really need to call your grandma back and it's getting late, or guilty because you need to review those tricky spelling words with your child one more time.

I promise you the world won't fall apart; in fact, you will come "more together." You deserve to be alone for 30 minutes to soak and not be needed by anyone. When you add three cups of Epsom salt to your bath water, you will detox your body and lymphatic system, all while relaxing and clearing your mind and soothing your sore muscles. Baths help you to wind down and sleep better—just like they do for babies. So, baby yourself all in the name of sleep, detoxification, and relaxation because tomorrow is coming, ready or not.

BEACH

What is it about being at the beach that makes us chill out? Is it the healing salty water that gives us a glow like no spa treatment ever could? Is it the never-ending rhythmic lull of waves that calls us quietly and hypnotically to a place of deep rest? Is it being barefoot on the sand that brings out our inner child as we write our names in the sand? Is it the sound of seagulls as they fly, chase, eat, float, and occasionally poop a little too close to our comfort zone? Is it styling our salty, wind-blown beach hair so that it always looks great? Is it realizing that every tiny broken shell was once home to some of God's most adaptable creatures—creatures not unlike ourselves that had to find change in order to live? Is it constructing a sandcastle with a moat and tower and imagining ourselves like Rapunzel (but in this fairytale, we are our own rescuer!)—all while hoping the whole lot doesn't get washed out by the incoming tide? Is it witnessing the strength of the Earth and its ability to provide all living things with what is needed to survive? Or is it pondering endless possibilities as we watch the sun rise over a horizon with the promise of a new day, every day. Or just maybe it's us enveloped in nature just as humans are designed to be— imperfectly perfect just for being us, sand in our butt cracks and all.

BEDTIME

We get so hung up on what society tells us about bedtime, and the topic becomes just another thing in our lives that makes us feel guilty. Maybe we use earplugs if our spouse snores or listen to a sound machine in order to fall asleep. Maybe we take prescription sleep drugs in order to stay in the marital bed because society says its "wrong" to leave the marital bedroom. Or "they" say it's wrong to sleep with our child cuddled up next to us, or to fall asleep with the TV on. Maybe it's time to stop listening to what "they" say and start listening to ourselves.

Now's the time to free yourself from society's confines of what is supposedly right and what is supposedly wrong, and just do what works for you! If, in order to get deep, restorative sleep, you need to move to the guestroom because of your spouse's snoring, then do it! If you fall asleep with the TV on, fine. If you would rather have your child in bed with you rather than get up four times to check on her fever, then do it. If you and your baby get deep, happy, restful sleep together during a thunderstorm, then perfect. If your child is in a phase where he just wants to be with you, then rock on. If the old sofa is better than sleeping next to a mean person, then grab blankets and go! This too shall pass.

Or you can look at it another way: All those fantastic nutrients that we eat during the day work their magic while we are sleeping. Our liver kicks in about 3:00 a.m. like the midnight-shift janitor cleaning the halls of an office building. If we are not sleeping, our livers cannot function properly to help us detox from the onslaught of daily toxins. So, the next time you secretly want to curl up on the sofa downstairs, go to the guestroom, or sleep with junior, just do it. In a perfect world it would be great to have babies who sleep deeply in their own beds while we make mad crazy love with our spouse and fall asleep in each other's arms only to awaken to the soft sound of *I Love You*s accompanied by the perfect cup of coffee and a rose freshly picked from the garden. That is a different book entirely, and written by someone else for sure. So, tonight what do you need to do to get some sleep? I give you permission to hit the snooze button on guilty thoughts about what a bad wife or mom you are, and just call it a night already.

BREATHE

Faith Hill said it best: just *breathe.* I can't stress enough the importance of breathing. I don't mean unconscious breathing through business meetings and traffic jams; I mean deep, therapeutic breathing. That's the kind of deep breathing that calms you down, lowers your blood pressure, and even helps you sleep better. It activates your relaxation system and quiets your mind and nerves. When we inhale, our stomachs are supposed to inflate, yet by bad habits, they go in. Here's a little exercise: Take a six-second inhale and inflate your stomach, not your chest. Then exhale for six seconds. Your stomach should go in toward your spine. It may feel super strange at first, and oddly enough, you may feel out of breath. But the more you do it, the better you'll feel. Do this a few times every morning and evening. And if you need more proof that this is the right way to breathe, just watch an infant sleeping. They do it right!

When I first started to be aware of my breathing, I was a non-believer, too, but I had to find ways to cope with the crazy people in my life. Practicing yoga also has helped me learn to breathe because yoga is the union of breath and body. You are the breath of life; without breath there is no life. Love yourself to health by beginning with your breath, your very life force.

C

You've probably guessed by now that I'm certainly not one of those ultra-health folks who say that in order to live a healthy lifestyle, you should eschew every indulgence of life. *Chocolate* and *coffee*, for instance—these are things that are best enjoyed in moderation. Same goes for *crying*, in my opinion. But open-flame *candles*? Bring them on. *Cuddle* time? The more the better. A good *counselor* to help you along the way? Oh yeah. Meditating at *church*? Absolutely. A clean and orderly living space? Sure, why not? A happy *career* path to validate your well-being? Heck yes! A meal that you cook in your own space to nourish your body and mind? It's on! Ponder these topics and start to dig a little deeper into who you are today and who you want to become tomorrow.

CANDLES

I light candles every single day. Doing so helps make my home a sanctuary and a getaway from the hustle-bustle of the horn-honking world. They smell good, too (see *Aromatherapy*), and help me find my happy place when the world around me is anything but. Sometimes, it's not even about the smell. I regularly purchase the religious candles from Walmart®, too. I like the Blessed Mother one because she's got my back on days it seems no one else does.

It took me a while to get into the candle habit but once I did, something always seems a little off when I don't have one lit. I look for soy or beeswax candles and ones without lead wire in the wicks because they are less toxic to inhale. If you're burning candles daily, go for natural ones, unless, of course, you want to breathe in neurotoxins. You can find natural candles at Whole

Foods Market®, Home Goods®, TJ Maxx®, and spas. Light a candle and slow down. On the kitchen counter, in the bedroom, or on the side of the bathtub—these are all great places for a little light. Stop equating candles with romantic love and start lighting them to celebrate self-love.

CAREER

There are jobs and there are careers. I venture to say that most Americans are working at jobs—you know, the salt mines you go to as a way to pay the bills, provide for your family, and get what is needed for those you are responsible for. Add to that things like vacations, airline tickets to go see the family, haircuts, or lunch with a friend, and you'll have more reasons of why you work. A job, to me, implies a "punch in, punch out" sort of mentality, whereas a career implies that your work inspires you and you have worked toward this position for a good part of your adult life.

I am Gemini, and as astrology would have it, I can be somewhat diverse. One book I read says that Gemini wives make the best wives because there are five women housed up in one body. That also applies to the career department. I've scooped ice cream, sold women's apparel, hawked gift shop goods, booked vacations as a travel agent, sold and marketed pharmaceutical software, worked as an assistant project manager in clinical operations, and finally, became a Certified Health Coach. You know what? Each and every job was perfect for me because they all satisfied a piece of Jeanine. I enjoy working with people, I love travel, and I love ice cream!

But having a career doesn't mean you need to sacrifice what's important to you. I once turned down what would have been a very great career opportunity...for someone else. On paper it was ideal. The salary, the title, and the prestigious company were all very enticing. I went on three interviews, endured drug testing, had the offer Federal Expressed to me...but I had a brick the size of Texas in my stomach. It was then that I really considered the reality: the commute to and from work, the traffic, the already stressed marriage, and the little time I would have had left to my day to prepare dinner, assist with homework, tackle bed time, and enjoy my kids. I thought about what that paycheck would "cost" me, and even though I tried to justify it, I couldn't. It was a very pivotal moment for me when I called the hiring manager and declined.

That very day I signed up for classes to become a Certified Health Coach. The application fee was $350. Later that day when I got my mail, I received a check from Blue Cross® Blue Shield® for $350. They had over charged me. Have you ever gotten an unexpected refund from your health insurance company? They're as rare as unicorn sightings! I took this as a sign that I was going in the perfect direction. I have always been deeply interested in wellness ever since I was in a car wreck on my junior prom night. The subsequent health complications I've had my entire life from that wreck only reinforced my passion for good health.

So here I am in a career I love. I am helping all sorts of shapes, sizes, and personalities fall in love …with themselves! Don't be afraid to take the leap if you're in a job you dislike. The next trapeze bar is there, you just need to put your arms out and have faith. If all else fails, you'll at least have the experience of trying to reach a little higher. It's a new day. How do you want to make a buck? What does making a buck cost your home life? What does it cost your health?

CHOCOLATE

Every so often, life calls for a little chocolate. As I sit here, a tad "PMSy" and writing, I have a scoop of Trader Joe's chocolate ice cream in front of me. I can't say I am a chocoholic, but I confess that sometimes it hits the spot like nothing else. As a kid, my favorite was Reese's Peanut Butter Cups. I could devour those two cups without thinking twice. Today, they still taste amazing and give me what my taste buds are whining for, but they also take me back to being 10 years old, sitting on my grandma's couch eating the treats that she got for me and each of my sisters. That, Bella, is not just chocolate—that is the ultimate in soul food.

Raw chocolate actually looks like a coffee bean and is full of antioxidants and magnesium. It also has zero sugar. During processing, companies add all sorts of emulsifiers, milk, sugar, and other chemicals to turn an innocent, healthy little bean into a candy bar. So my rule for chocolate is to choose the highest percentage dark you can find. Check out www.sunfood.com for lots of raw chocolate products. Like any treat, a little candy bar is okay at Halloween or a scoop of ice cream is great once in a while on a hot summer day or movie night, but remember, a little goes a long way. It's fine to enjoy hot and gooey s'mores around the fire pit surrounded by friends on a fall evening, but it's not something I'd recommend doing daily. Pitch, or better yet, stop buying the crappy, cheap, overprocessed chocolate snacks, and savor the good ones—the ones that feed your soul while you eat them. Avoid the processed chocolate that causes you to gain weight as you mindlessly eat five more cookies than you planned on. When your body is in survival mode, eating unhealthy treats makes you feel bad and look worse. You need to choose real foods for real living. Junk in, junk out!

CHURCH

The older I get the more I enjoy celebrating mass at my church. I am no longer that young girl who cares about how her voice sounds when she sings, and my intense yoga practice has taught me how to quiet my mind and be present and keep an open heart for God. Whatever your own spiritual and religious beliefs are, you may want to experiment with finding a church that feels like a family. It is a beautiful thing when people come together with common beliefs and celebrate something larger than just themselves. It's a place to learn, to be present, and to be surrounded by others who are making a choice to grow their faith. Maybe now is a good time to free yourself from what you think you should do, and just follow your open and spiritual self through another door to another church.

Your spiritual self needs nourishing just like your physical self. What feels right to you?

CLEAN

Remember when I told you I was a Gemini and that I was five wives rolled into one? None of those wives like house cleaning. I do, however, love my surroundings clean and orderly. If given the choice between making the bed or going to yoga, I would definitely squeeze in a yoga class. But all in all, I don't thrive in clutter, and the older I get the more I like things orderly. When women are pregnant, they nest: fix up the house, wash clothes, vacuum in places they haven't cleaned in forever. And to a degree, when I am hormonal, I tend to do that, too. That is a biological and instinctual need to fluff the nest. If you ever feel that way, just go with it. You may feel an all new sense of calm just from a little Windex, paper towels, and the vacuum. When your life seems out of control, sometimes it's a good outlet to start scrubbing and organizing. It helps to bring order to a chaotic situation. It is also very good for the soul to donate a few bags of outgrown clothes for the neighbors, or bring a few bags to your favorite local charity. Everybody wins!

Since you can't lock out those toxic people, clean up your living space as much as possible and let in your calm.

Jeanine Finelli

COFFEE

(Sing to the tune of "Oh Where, Oh Where Has My Little Dog Gone.")

Oh where, oh where do I begin to tell you

how much I lo-o-ve my beans?

I don't need eight cups or even three

But without one, I may get really mean!

Caffeine is a legal addiction and a multibillion-dollar industry. I find it ironic that our nation runs on coffee yet sleeping pills are among the most prescribed medicines. Ever notice how our nation's kids are the target of cleverly marketed "energy" drinks that are sold in shiny and cool cans? Somewhere a team of individuals is sitting around a conference table desperately trying to figure out *how* to get our kids addicted to caffeine. If they succeed with these energy drinks, they have secured the next generation of coffee house addicts. It's a sweet deal for them, but not for our children.

Coffee beans have been harvested for thousands of years, and they actually do pack a powerful antioxidant punch. Caffeine is helpful in alleviating things like migraines and, of course, can make you feel more alert. Years ago if you told me that I had to leave at 6:00 a.m. to drive to my son's soccer game two hours away and not have any coffee, I would have probably hit you over the head and taken yours! Today, I manage it a little better and have one cup a day in the morning. That one cup is strictly my alone time—I savor the comfort and routine of my morning quiet time before the hustle-bustle of the day begins. As babies, we were conditioned to crave a warm, creamy liquid to sooth us, be it a breast or a bottle. Think of soul foods like cappuccino, hot chocolate, or tea—they are relaxing to our nerves. That probably means we shouldn't be running around like crazy ladies when we are drinking them.

21

It's good to take a caffeine break every now and again. I detox periodically from coffee, and it is torture for me at first. And like any addiction, I suffer from withdrawal symptoms. Even though I only have one cup a day, when I detox for a week to a month, I initially get a headache, become a little crabby, and also have some insomnia. After about four days, it gets so much better, and I have *more* energy and sleep better. If you're planning a coffee vacation, pick a time when you don't have major stress in your life—that may not be the best time to pass on the morning cup of sanity.

The problem with coffee addiction involves the adrenal glands. Caffeine tells your adrenal glands to take a nap. Your adrenals are responsible for producing sex, energy, and stress hormones. The more coffee they get, the more they are like, *Lady, you're on your own. Make your own darn energy. We're going back to sleep!* When you take their coffee boost away and give up caffeine, they get pissed because now they have to go back to work, and they have forgotten how, thanks to you and your predictable surge of artificial energy. It is similar to overusing antibiotics: The more you take, the less your immune system fights for you because it wants the antibiotics to do its dirty work.

When you drink coffee throughout the day and the buzz wears off, your adrenals turn into screaming babies that need more, more, more! When they don't get more, they get exhausted, which means you have no energy, and then you reach for another cup. It's a vicious cycle. So whether you have one cup or ten, the addiction is real. Of course less is better, but here is how to have the healthiest cup of coffee in the morning:

- Drink 10 ounces of lemon water first. This detoxes your liver and creates an alkalized state before the onslaught of acid.

- Choose organic coffee and reduce more than 30 pesticides, herbicides, and fungicides from your cup.

- Drink it black! If you use creamer, use half and half, almond, or coconut milk, and don't add extra sugar. If you need some sweetness, try a tad of an all-natural sweetened creamer. Typical creamers contain a ton of sugar and those dreaded transfats, among other things. One serving generally has more than one teaspoon of sugar. If you're using two or three servings, that is 16 plus grams of sugar (equal to four teaspoons!) just in your morning coffee. Try liquid stevia or Monk fruit instead.

As you can see, the bean itself isn't bad. It is the quantity and how we prepare it that turns it into a 400-calorie, adrenal killing, mood altering, sleep robbing drug that's innocently disguised in the mug your six-year-old decorated for you last Mother's Day. Experiment with a two-week coffee cleanse, and if you can't go "cold Kona," then replace it with a cup of green tea. It still has caffeine, but is also super high in antioxidants and contains zero calories. More importantly, never buy your children energy drinks...ever!

COOK

You know from my story about growing up in an Italian family that food is body and soul nourishment, and so it should come as no surprise that I enjoy creating meals for those I love. But cooking sometimes can put you in a vulnerable place. Suppose you're cooking dinner for eight guests. You put out the china, clean the wine glasses until they sparkle, fold the napkins, and light the candles so your table looks like it's right out of a Disney fairytale. You sit down to dine and...the roast is dry, the mashed potatoes are runny, the chocolate soufflé is flat, and the roasted veggies are way too salty. Big bummer! Do yourself a favor and find a few dishes that you enjoy cooking *and* eating. Perfect them, and make them your go-to meals. I love the recipes at www.cleaneating.com. They are just as yummy as they are healthy.

Sometimes life calls for quick. My quick is a frozen pizza to which I add lots of veggies and make a big side salad. Sometimes quick is an omelet with cheese and veggies—who doesn't love breakfast for dinner? Cooking takes a little prep and awareness; the kitchen, after all, is the heart of your home where everyone gathers. Invest a little money in good pots and pans, utensils, spices, and quality ingredients. Cook when you have time so it doesn't feel like a chore, and make extra for lunches during the week.

An exhausting day at the office followed by an evening of carpooling three kids around to three different activities may not be the best night to cook. You want to keep things as low-stress as possible by planning ahead a little. Fill your Crockpot® with veggies, broth, and chicken for a yummy hot stew that greets you when you get home. Swing by the store for a roasted chicken and prepare some sweet potato fries and steamed broccoli. *Voilà!* Dinner is served, and you haven't lost your mind in the process. Life is about simplifying where you can and feeling guilt-free about it. *Buon appetito!*

COUNSELOR

Sometimes we could all benefit from a little good guidance in life. We are not experts in everything, and it's certainly difficult to see the forest for the trees when we're feeling vulnerable and afraid. Similar to finding a good doctor or lawyer, finding the right counselor is also a trial and error process.

When you are seeking clarity, tools for sanity, and healthy progress, you have to be sure that you are placing your mental well-being in capable hands. Ask around, do some research, and find out who is in your insurance network. Schedule an appointment and see if the counselor understands the magnitude of *your* situation. Listen carefully to what your intuition or gut instincts tell you. Does the counselor understand your pain? Is she listening with a fresh and open brain, or does she seem preoccupied? Does he look into your eyes and really listen? Does she seem jaded and detached when tears well up in your eyes? Do you have to ask for a tissue because he is unphased by the snot running down your nose as you tell your innermost painful thoughts? It takes time to find Mr. or Ms. Right Counselor.

I have found that over the years, several counselors I visited were neither a good fit for me nor my children. It was my experience that either the counselor was too young and wanted to provide a textbook session using tools that I already tried, or they were so seasoned that they had fallen into a groove where they seemed to have lost the ability to be objective. It felt like they just wanted to prescribe a dose of "hug it out" and "this too shall pass."

Life is filled with people who don't listen and talk way too much about themselves. A competent counselor will listen more, talk less, hand you tissues, and give you tools to fill your bag with ways to cope when situations arise. He or she won't just sit there and let you vent as if that's all you needed. You need healing, so be very cautious of who you place in that role. The wrong counselor will keep getting co-pays, and your tool kit will remain empty. You may ask yourself if you are any better off than you were six months ago. If the answer is no, then grab your purse and say *ciao!*

CRY

I am a big proponent of a good cry. I am the girl who cries over sad movies, sad songs, and when I really miss someone I love. I cry when I watch my kids open presents on Christmas morning, and I cry when someone I love is crying. Although I have a pretty high threshold for physical pain—I gave birth to two children without drugs, have had multiple surgeries resulting from a severe auto accident that almost killed me on prom night, have gotten tattoos, have stubbed toes (who hasn't?), and been stung by many bees at once—I guess you could say my crying is the result of a deep emotional stirring.

Like you, I have gotten my feelings so hurt that I had no idea that type of emotional, gut-wrenching, agonizing pain was even possible. The despair that goes with constant betrayal and the feeling of someone greedily taking something that isn't theirs to take surely creates a gorge in your heart. Surprisingly, the gorge can always run just a little bit deeper, and has the potential to create sharp edges that get etched into the wall of your ticker. So the next time you need a release of pain that you feel is welled up inside, let it out. Watch a sad movie or listen to that sad love song. Your eyes will be a little red and puffy that day, but afterward it's funny how much more clearly and brightly you will see. My blue eyes always seem a little bluer the day after, and so, a good cry isn't so bad after all.

So go ahead and release the emotions, cleanse the tear ducts, and brighten those beautiful eyes of yours because you've got to let the pain out where you can. Hang up your superwoman cape for a day, and let the tears flow.

CUDDLE

Thank you to my spectacular daughter for always reminding me of the power of a cuddle. She exhibits one of the greatest examples of love for animals I have ever seen despite her terrible allergies to all things furry. She wants to cuddle with practically all living things, up to and including the copperhead we found on the driveway. This love of life is very real to her. In first grade, she witnessed a classmate killing a grasshopper. She was consumed by this insect assault for the rest of the day. Another time, she wept for an hour because we had to pitch my son's leftover calamari after it sat in the hot car too long while we enjoyed gelato. She sobbed, "The poor little squid died for nothing!" Where most people would never think like this, she does.

In lieu of cuddling a furry pet, we instead cuddle on the couch with all the Build-a-Bears and American Girl dolls, and of course her favorite, Ducky. We'll make snacks and put on our matching jammies, and she will curl up on my lap even though there are three other places to sit. It's her way of sharing her love.

So make time to cuddle your children, hold your aging mother's hand, snuggle with that puppy or kitten, or maybe just hug that stuffed animal that's been through it all with you. Cuddling means you aren't driving, cooking, or working. You are just being loved and giving love, and love is kind.

D

D is for taking a deeper look into what you want your health makeover to include. Does it include using natural products on your body like aluminum-free *deodorant*? Could it be going on a *date*? It doesn't even have to be something you do. It could be someone you know. In your life, who has influenced you for the better? Could it be your *dad* or your *daughter* or your *doctor*? How do you find what makes you happy? Is it visualizing a favorite place (*Il Duomo*) that brings to mind a happy memory? Or perhaps it's cranking up some tunes and *dancing*?

DAD

If you want to know the measure of a man, ask his family. Those who have relied on him and those who learned from his example are the best ones to ask. He leaves a fortuitous legacy of love, truth, and manhood to his children and grandchildren.

No word in the galaxy could ever capture the essence of how I feel about my dad. My father is peaceful but not a pushover, and a lover not a fighter—unless it means fighting for the well-being of those he adores and protects. I could write a book just about him. He is the reason I have not settled for less. As difficult as my journey has been, had I not known how things could be, I think I would have settled for *unkind love*. Dad, you rock, you are the rock, and you are the reason I never threw in the towel and settled for 90 percent of what's out there. I know there is more, thanks to you. You have loved, cherished, and honored my Mommy. I saw the love and respect you gave to her, and I know better.

Who's your Dad or your male, loving guidance? What do you love about him? What are the gifts and lessons he leaves you with?

DANCE

When I think of dancing, I think of my dad and my daughter. By watching my father, I learned how to dance, and as I shared with you in the prologue of this book. As kids, my sisters and I would take turns standing on his feet and dance. Dancing was abundant in my childhood home. It was so much fun! My parents were always the first ones out on any dance floor at weddings. Others would join after watching them swirl and twirl around the dance floor; my parents always had a ball dancing together. When dancing with a partner, it's impossible to make someone look silly without looking silly yourself; therefore, it's a team effort.

Summer 2012 was a pivotal one for me. For nine days, my kids and I had so much fun together with my extended family in New York. On that trip I downloaded a song—"I Love How You Love Me"— that reminds me of my grandmother because she always liked Jerry Vale. But for the first time ever, I really listened to words. Right then and there I decided that it was one of the most romantic songs I had ever heard. So in my parent's kitchen I played it, and my father came into the room and danced with me. I hadn't danced with a man in years. My marriage was so void of anything romantic and intimate that I had forgotten what it felt like to dance. I realized that just because one man didn't want to dance with me—the one man I *thought* really should want to—didn't mean that I couldn't enjoy the fulfillment of dancing with those I love. In fact, I learned that those dances were more than I could have hoped for.

Fast forward to now. My daughter Lily and I dance a lot these days. We dance while *Dancing with the Stars* is on, and we put on my favorite playlist and dance to that, too. We slow dance, silly dance, dance the Can Can, and make up a few moves of our own. I absolutely cherish this time with her more than words can say. I remember dancing with my son Domenic when he was just three months old. I am so thankful for the love of my children and for all of the joyful dances they have given me.

So, do you like to dance? When was the last time you put on an oldie but goodie and just let it all out? How about dancing lessons? You don't have two left feet; you are quite possibly just in wrong and boring company.

DATE

Not much to report here, folks. All I can say is try to have fun, but keep your boundaries intact. Don't listen to others who tell you to get out there if you're not ready to. Pay attention to what your gut tells you and don't put anyone before your kids! They have been through too much and need your time and attention more than ever. Let the decisions be your own, not someone else's. Stay whole, healthy, and intact because you have been to hell and back. Your future awaits, and you're the author of your life story. When the right person comes into your life, quite unexpectedly, you will be ready for more because you know your own heart better than anyone else. Until then, light a candle for yourself and poke around on Netflix.

DAUGHTER

There's such promise of new life and possibility when you hold your baby girl and look into her eyes for the first time.

My Lilybelle, where do I begin? I am so glad you picked me to be your mother. You are hope when I feel there is none, a speck of light when I think the world is dark. Your laugh makes me feel alive and your touch reminds me I am already perfect. I love our time together whether we are walking in the woods, watching *Nick Jr.,* or doing math homework. Every day of being with you is like winning the lottery, and my heart holds immeasurable amounts of awe for you. Live your life, see the world, do unto others as you would have them do unto you, but don't take any crap from anyone that assaults your soul. Believe in yourself like I believe in you…no matter what is said or done to you, ever!

DEODORANT

As women, we aren't supposed to have wrinkles, gray hair, pores, cellulite, saggy boobs, laugh lines, or gas. And just forget about sweating! I call BS on this because the most gorgeous women I have ever seen were in Italy where natural beauty abounds. Yes, of course, youth can be simply stunning, but I think the most beautiful women are the older Italian ladies who never wear makeup or, no doubt, underarm deodorant.

A few years back, I wandered around the grounds of San Spirito in Florence with my parents and my daughter. Outside the church was a plaza, complete with pigeons, a breeze, local arts for sale, and a bench with five old ladies on it. They reminded me so much of my Great Grandma Irene from Italy. These women weren't skinny, and their faces showed lines etched from decades of laughter, hard work, and tears. They were beautiful women who were real. And I'll take the bet that they didn't use underarm deodorant to stave off something as natural as sweat.

Imagine shaving your underarms then putting a layer of chemicals on your tender, broken skin—skin that happens to be dangerously close to your lymphatic system. Conventional deodorants usually contain aluminum, which works by blocking your sweat glands so you don't perspire. Perspiration is your body's way of cooling off and ridding your body of excess toxins. And remember, your skin absorbs what you put on it. Why would you slowly poison yourself for beauty? I think every woman should use a natural line of deodorant free of PEGs, parabens, petrochemicals, aluminum compounds, and antibacterials. The problems are that many brands simply don't

31

work, and body chemistry differs among people so you may have to try a few brands to find the one that's best for you.

I love Pristine Beauty® deodorant, which is made in Raleigh by a lovely lady, Blaire Kessler, who is also a breast cancer survivor (www.shoppristinebeauty.com). Her "pit tip" is that it can take up to three weeks for your body to adapt to using a new deodorant, so be patient. *Aluminum chlorohydrate* is the chemical ingredient that is typically used in antiperspirants to reduce sweating, and since Blaire's line is free of toxins, feel free to dust a bit of baking soda under your arm after you apply her Take a Whiff!® So stop poisoning yourself and remember that real women sweat.

DOCTOR

Fortune smiled upon me when I found my doctor, whom I presently work for. Years ago, he was the only one who listened to me and made sense of all that was going on with my health, when other doctors told me I was hormonal, or I was overreacting, or it was my appendix. In 1999, I spiked a 106-degree fever, and the surgeon removed my appendix only to find it was perfectly fine; he never figured out what was causing my intense, life-threatening illness. My new doctor said let's figure this out, and I'm happy to say that he did. Thanks to him, I understand my body better and live as vibrantly as I can. I never would have guessed that my near-fatal car accident on May 13, 1988, would have sparked my never-ending journey toward optimal health and would inspire me to help others.

Finding a great doctor proves to be a difficult task these days. With pressures mounting in the medical community, patients are getting less and less one-on-one time with their health care provider, less insurance coverage that they pay more for, and more prescriptions. I urge you to learn as much as you can and find a doctor who welcomes your questions and insight. Keep researching until you find one who is focused on prevention and whole-person wellness. A competent doctor will discuss stress from your abusive marriage and even put you in touch with a therapist, or at the very least show you there is a connection between your depression and your negative and unfaithful spouse. A not-so-great doctor will write you a prescription for sleeping pills or antidepressants, and send you on your merry way.

Ask friends, coworkers, and like-minded people who they use and why. Meet the doctor and pay for a consult. If you aren't "feeling the love," then don't go back. Why do we trust our most prized possessions (brain, heart, body) with just anyone? Steer clear of doctors who are intimidated by your knowledge and passion for prevention. It may take a little time to investigate, but why leave an important job in the hands of just any doctor? Ask around, get some feedback, and make an appointment. Your health is non-negotiable.

DUOMO

Where is your happy place? You know the one I'm talking about—the one where you can go in a New York minute without ever leaving your house? Il Duomo in Florence, Italy, is one of mine. I can go there in a heartbeat. When mean words are being said to me, I go there. I go there in my head by putting in my *Sounds of Tuscany* CD.

I chose to fill my mind with images of me and my parents and daughter standing outside the massive red Duomo of Santa Maria Del Fiore. No matter where you are in the city on the shores of the Arno River, you can spot it. I have paintings of it in my home, and I can hear its church bells ringing through every corridor of my heart. Lily was so fascinated by it that three weeks later when it was her birthday, she wanted a Duomo cake, complete with baby animals and fall leaves—all her favorite things.

So where is it? Go there in your mind and tune out the negativity. I promise you this helps heal and helps you to just get through the day with one precious memory at a time. Those memories are yours and yours alone.

E

As I go through each letter, I'm sharing with you what I consider important items and thoughts to consider that helped me when I wasn't at my best. Does your *ego* boost you up or get you into trouble? Do you have enough *energy* to get you through the day? When was the last time you took a bath with *Epsom salt* sprinkled in? Have you ever tried *essential oils* to perk up listless skin or mood? Have you considered the influence of *evolution*—and I'm not talking Darwin here!—has on your daily existence? How do you fit *exercise* into your life—or do you? As you read through the *E* section, consider how each item can influence how you feel as you go through your day.

EGO

We all have one, and you shouldn't feel guilty about it. It's not always a bad thing. What isn't so cool is when you live in your ego and not your soul. I bet you can think of someone right now who always needs his or her ego stroked. I like to think that my ego and soul work in tandem—my ego gives me a boost when I need one, and my soul makes sure I don't go too high. When you are in a tough situation where a decision needs to be made, ask yourself if you are feeding your ego or feeding your soul.

For example, maybe you were dating a man who told you awful things and never wanted to spend time with you. Your ego may have responded with a big fat *screw you!* But then along comes that guy who you know is sweet on you. You drink in all of his compliments and appreciate the idiosyncrasy of being made to feel like a million bucks from someone you barely even know. Your ego, tipsy on wine, accepts his invitation back to his place and you let whatever happens happen. Your soul might whisper to you that you *already* know that you are a fun-loving, sexy woman and that you really don't need a fantastic kisser to validate that. Just remember that every choice has a price tag— the highest being your integrity. Is anyone really worth compromising that for?

One of the reasons I love practicing yoga is because in most studios there are few big egos. It's quite possible that I'm so blissed out I don't even notice them. It's been my experience that, unlike in gyms where members strut like peacocks, the yoga studio is more of a competitive- and judgment-free zone. Take the occasional dip into the ego pool but make sure that your soul will not be negatively challenged by it. Regardless of what choices you make—and I pass no judgment on what you need to heal—*don't let those decisions change your core or set you back from where you want to be*. You have already been through so much soul evolution, and no ego boost is worth chipping away at what you have built. Always honor your soul first before your ego and you will be moving in the right direction…great kisses or not.

ENERGY

When I watch my daughter go for hours playing, running, swimming, and laughing, I marvel at the constant flow of energy she has. Sometimes I wish I could get just a pinch of it. The truth is that we *can* feel that alive even though we may feel chewed up and spit out. As we age, chronic stress and hormone fluctuations beat the heck out of our human growth hormone reserves, and restoring our energy just takes a tad more awareness now. We are no longer those effortlessly energized children. A step in the right direction would be detoxifying from negative people who zap our energy just by being around them. (I know you are with me on this one! Bravo to you for making the decision to choose health and detox from energy-suckers!) Energizing ourselves also requires a delicate balance of getting enough restorative sleep; maintaining a healthy diet of fruits, vegetables, protein, and the right carbohydrates; and minimizing caffeine, sugar, and alcohol.

When it comes to foods, I find that the energy is in the color. Think *rainbow* when you eat, and consider how much color is on your plate. Can you add berries to your cereal or smoothie? Can you add cucumber and avocado to your turkey sandwich? Can you double your salad with dinner? These colorful foods are filled with vitamins and minerals, and can even oxygenate us and lift our moods and spirits. How do you feel after eating a steak and baked potato versus a salad with tofu or grilled chicken? Did you know that approximately 80 percent of our energy will go toward digesting such a large dose of animal protein and carbohydrates? That's often why after a big meal you wind up lying on the couch waving the white flag. Smoothies are awesome for quick bioavailability of nutrients and they don't require a ton of energy in order to be digested. Here is my favorite go-to morning smoothie recipe:

Morning Smoothie

- 1 scoop Vega® protein or Garden of Life® raw protein
- ¼ banana
- 1 cup blueberries and raspberries (frozen)
- ½ cup frozen kale
- 1 cup unsweetened vanilla almond milk
- some water

Add all ingredients to a blender and give it a whirl. Add water to achieve your desired consistency. Yummy!

EPSOM SALT

Granny was right. Epsom salt baths really are good for us. Epsom salt is magnesium and magnesium is an amazing mineral; it's also the one we tend to be most deficient in. Added to a warm bath, the salt will dissolve, and will be absorbed into the skin to soften tired, achy muscles and help to open the pores and rid your body of icky stuff. It's a great idea to take a soak if you feel under the weather, or perhaps if your coworker has been sneezing and coughing over the cubicle wall all week! The salt is a fantastic exfoliator for dry skin. Epsom salt even can be mixed with water and used internally as a laxative. It tastes horrible, but it works. The benefits are many.

I can't really talk about Epsom salt without touching on skin (pun intended). Never use colored or scented salts unless they are completely organic with all natural essential oils. Most products contain too many artificial colors and scents and that, Bella, is bad for your skin. Baths are supposed to make you clean! Reduce your toxic load by treating your skin with love. Remember, your skin is your body's largest organ and what you put on your skin goes into your blood, liver, and other organs. You are choosing to live vibrantly and healthfully, so why would you want to slather your skin with toxins from makeup, shampoo, and lotions?

ESSENTIAL OILS

Our sense of smell is a powerful thing. It can have an effect on how we perceive, experience, and remember things. I touched on this in *Aromatherapy*. I guess that's why essential oils play a huge role in aiding my mental clarity and calmness. There are countless brands to choose from ranging from very synthetic to extremely pure. There are hundreds of single oil blends such as lavender, basil, cinnamon, and pine, and also multi-oil blends with names like inner child, gratitude, and sacred mountain. Essential oils are the "blood" of the plant, and have various uses in homeopathic medicine and healing. When you're feeling the effects of a stressful, toxic relationship, sometimes a little pick-me-up can be just what you need.

Shop online or visit local health food stores to learn more about what lines they carry and what each oil can do for you. I recommend only the purest oils because many of the less expensive ones are made with synthetic ingredients, and remember, your skin is your largest organ that absorbs everything you put on it. It wouldn't be terribly healthy to inhale synthetic vapors into your lungs either (think air fresheners or cheap scented candles). When shopping, look for pharmaceutical grade and organic oils that can be ingested as well as burned in a diffuser.

You can use ones like oregano and ginger internally for detoxification by adding drops to water or directly into your food. Or use just a few drops of something like frankincense on the crown of your head, on your wrists, or on the soles of your feet to lift your spirits and calm your rattled nerves. Peppermint is a favorite oil of mine. It's very cooling and refreshing. It's ultra pure and potent, and one drop is equal to the peppermint in about 20 bags of peppermint tea. One deep whiff of the oil can wake you up and bring mental clarity, a few deep whiffs can knock out a headache, and four or five drops rubbed into the bottoms of your feet can reduce a fever. Who knew?

I like products infused with oils from Young Living™ (www.youngliving.com), such as lotions, vitamin capsules, shampoos, toothpastes, and more. The Thieves® line of products is wonderful for boosting the immune system and working to combat viruses and especially respiratory issues. I carry it in my purse and breathe it in on airplanes to help keep germs at bay while I'm flying. The scent is clove and cinnamon and smells so invigorating! There is an oil for every reason and every season. Sniff away and bring more strength, health, and clarity into your day.

EVOLUTION

Cinderella once sang, "Have faith in your dreams and someday, your rainbow will come shining through. No matter how your heart is grieving, if you keep on believing, the dream that you wish will come true." Truer words were never spoken. Like Cinderella, your unhappiness is temporary. Growing emotionally can be a horrible experience—until you can be far enough along to look back at what the purpose of your pain was. You are evolving right now. We all are like a rough, little grain of sand inside the oyster shell that someday will become a smooth and shiny pearl. Your heart may feel broken and be pounding out of your chest, but your spirit is becoming stronger, despite not knowing what lies ahead for you. Trust in the process that you, too, are being molded and shaped into a one-of-a-kind pearl. You are evolving into the person you are meant to be— challenges, smiles, heartbreak, and all. You can do this, Bella!

EXERCISE

All of the organic and healthy food in the world cannot replace the need for exercising regularly. Exercise plays an important role in your mood, cravings, sleep, bone density, hormones, weight, cardiovascular health, and how much you love or hate your butt! Think about it...our ancestors were constantly foraging, hunting, walking, and climbing, and were probably much more fit than modern man in order to escape wild animals and enemies. Our bodies are designed for constant movement, yet with today's sedentary lifestyle of working office jobs, taking care of our families, and tending to life in general, our days have precious little time for squeezing in exercise. Throw in managing a stressful, toxic relationship, and you have a recipe for ill health. What has happened to us as a nation? We love to watch dancing shows, but rarely dance. We love to watch sports, but rarely throw a football with the kids. Stop the madness, and just do it already!

You don't even have to join an expensive gym. I am definitely one of those people who *hate* working out in the gym. For me, exercise is a balance of hot and power yoga, walking nature trails, and hiking. I shift my schedule around as needed for kids and work, but ultimately I am exercising at least four days a week. A yoga studio provides the perfect landscape for me to clear my mind, strengthen my bones, and shape my core. We tend to think that our only option is the gym, but far from it. Find something that inspires you to work hard and improve your flexibility. Sometimes even staying within the same activity but with a different teacher is enough to keep me coming back for more. Try an exercise video or go online to sample what's on YouTube! If you try a new activity and aren't feeling the love, just move on to something else. Better yet, go outside and take a walk with a friend. Mix it up and change it up, but get out there and get that heart rate up!

Here are my two simple exercise rules: be consistent and enjoy what you do. Consistent doesn't have to be rigid. Consistency is fitting exercise into your day where you can. Do you have an exercise routine? Do you enjoy it? If you're not a regular exerciser, start small. Review your calendar on Sunday and see where you can fit in some movement. Set a personal goal to work out two hours a week—spread out in 30-minute increments if you have to—then gradually increase your time. When life is stressful and your plate is full, exercise is key to your health and mental well-being. Without exercise, you will lose bone mass, and your body will quickly degenerate. Not good! Give your heart the gift of a daily workout so that it can support you in times of stress and exhaustion. Besides, healthy hearts fall out of fear and into love.

F

The *F*s cover a span of ideas and objects that, when I was in the throes of my toxic relationship, helped me keep it together. I would have been lost had it not been for my *friends* and exploring *forgiveness*. Well, forgiveness takes time, but you'll come around, just like I did. Even something simple like smelling fresh-cut *flowers* or walking outside to breathe in *fresh air* were sometimes enough to snap me out of a funk. Remembering to be kind to my body by eating more *fiber* helped a lot, too. *F* is also for freedom—as in freedom from feeling bad about yourself, freedom from unhappiness, freedom from a bad relationship. How can these concepts and things become your companions on your journey toward good mental, physical, and spiritual health?

FIBER

Eat more fiber. You've probably heard it before. But do you know why fiber is so good for your health?

Dietary fiber, also known as roughage, is found mainly in fruits, vegetables, whole grains, and legumes and is probably best known for its ability to prevent or relieve constipation. Feeling good and staying regular is only part of the story. A fiber rich diet can help with weight management, blood sugar stability, lowering cholesterol, and disease prevention. Fiber is big business with all sorts of fiber pills, drinks, and powders on the market, but as always, the best place to get fiber is from a whole foods diet. Fiber is the part of the plant that your body cannot absorb. It passes through your digestive system completely. When you use a juicer, you remove all fiber from the food so the nutrients are immediately bioavailable and don't need to travel through your body. When you blend or make a smoothie, you keep the fiber and it must travel through your intestines in order to absorb all the nutrients. There are two types of fiber—soluble and insoluble:

- **Soluble fiber:** This type of fiber dissolves in water to form a gel-like material. It can help lower blood cholesterol and glucose levels. It is found in beans, apples, oats, citrus, carrots, psyllium, and barley.

- **Insoluble fiber:** This type of fiber helps food to move through your digestive system and increases stool bulk, which is the fiber that helps relieve constipation. Good sources of insoluble fiber are wheat bran, beans, nuts, cruciferous vegetables, and potatoes.

A high-fiber diet is healthy because it normalizes bowel movements and helps to keep bowels free of toxins, lowers cholesterol, helps to manage blood sugar, and can help with weight loss. Fiber attaches to extra hormones, cholesterol, fat, and other toxins your body doesn't need. A small apple with the skin has about five grams of fiber; an adult woman needs about 20–30 grams of fiber a day.

You may be deficient in love and respect, but don't short change yourself where you don't need to. Fiber will help you feel full and satisfied when toxic people are depleting you of vital nutrients. After all, you need to be healthy so that you can move on with your life!

FLOWERS

Oftentimes in relationships that are destructive, flowers are accompanied by a note that reads "I'm sorry." It can be a love/hate sort of thing because the flowers are so gorgeous yet are a reminder—not an eraser—of pain endured. However, my parents used to send me gorgeous bouquets for various occasions and those always made my day brighter. As time went on, I began buying myself flowers. I even bought flowers for myself one wedding anniversary to celebrate "me" and my resilience. It is all about taking control, and loving yourself first, right? Why wait for someone to make you feel appreciated? You need to appreciate yourself and in time that will bring in others who appreciate you too. A small bouquet of fresh flowers brightens up any room and is a sign of life, color, and vibrancy. Of course, my favorite flower is the lily!

Don't underestimate the strength of pretty things like flowers…or yourself. Just think of the Lotus flower. This is one of the most incredibly resilient plants on earth. The lotus flower symbolizes an opening of the heart and perseverance because deep in the murky, muddy water of still lakes, the anchored root stretches triumphantly to the surface of the water. It is completely covered in mud and knows no way other than reaching up, up, up toward the light and warmth of the sun. When the flower reaches the surface, the layers open one by one. When this happens, every speck of dirt is magically washed away, and the flower settles at the top of the water representing eternity and love.

We all have our muck and dirt that anchors us down in life, and many times we find fascination in that filth. But like the lotus, we must remain deeply rooted in order to rise to the top. Those roots will ground us no matter what waters we must swim through on our way to opening our hearts. You *are* the lotus and you are just perfect. You will realize this. Keep looking up and you will see a clearing of warmth and safety to open up in, and at that moment you will have a perspective you never ever had from the bottom.

FORGIVENESS

When we are hurt, and thus living in our ego, forgiveness seems practically impossible. For me it was very difficult because every time I would forgive, the same thing would happen again, leaving me to feel like life's biggest loser. Forgiveness doesn't mean you have to keep accepting the behavior. It means that sometimes you need to walk away from an unhealthy situation and free your heart from holding on to resentment. I also read once that resentment is the pill you swallow hoping to make someone else sick. Boy, is that one true!

While the person who has betrayed or hurt you is sleeping well and going on with his life, you are left seething inside with a pit in your stomach. This can lead to overeating, gaining weight, and having high blood pressure because you are pissed off. Remember that your health is non-negotiable and you must protect it. Haven't you given enough already? Why throw your physical well-being into it after you have already been emotionally disabled?

It is so true that people put us down because they can. It's generally because they feel so insecure about *themselves*. It's interesting how many men (and maybe women, too) seek out loving, kind, and forgiving partners because they know that those types of personalities will overlook things for the good of the whole. I always find I am more resolute with forgiveness when I remember one thing: Jesus had thousands against him, and very few for him. I have so many people for me, and very few against me. If Jesus can persevere in truth, then without a doubt, I can, too. And when all else fails, remember *the first step to forgiveness may be realizing that the other person is an idiot!* I saw that on a button once.

So at the end of the day, I get forgiveness as a concept. It makes sense to me. For me though, forgiveness is knowing that my soul had some growing to do. I thank the Lord for allowing me to move past that person I was and grow into the one I want to be. What can you let go of *for your own healing*?

FRESH AIR

I revel in being outside and having the windows wide open. It's just another way I can feel Mother Nature's devotion for me.

Where I live in the south, it practically kills me that the pollen is horrible in spring and I can't really open the windows at all, and summer…well, just *fuhgeddaboudit*! During the fall, though, I open the windows as much as I can. When the sunlight reflects off of the colorful leaves, I just let it go, and I feel so relaxed. No matter what's going on around me, in that moment of fresh air surrounding me, I feel alive and am reminded that everything has a purpose. If your day is filled with angst, take a moment to step outside, close your eyes, and just take deep breaths to cleanse your lungs and fill you up with oxygen and calmness. It's the little things that keep us going. Or are those little things really the big things?

FRIEND

Friend is a word that seems to have become watered down in meaning these days. Thanks to Facebook, this topic is sort of linked to ego, and sadly, so much of our contact is seldom face-to-face. Who are your true friends? Steer clear of imposters. You are better off without them. Friends will never judge you when you are a sobbing mess trying to find your way through it all. When something devastating happens to you, that's exactly when you need to turn to those you trust the most.

I never would have made it through my toxic relationship had it not been for the friends who walked my journey of truth with me. They were there every day for me, and not just to let me vent. They helped me find solutions, ways, paths, and answers. They helped me brainstorm and plan, and they shared their brilliant ideas and kept me focused. When sleep was a stranger to me, when I was crying, when I had too much wine, when I needed more wine, when I needed to hear the truth, when I realized what was going on in my marriage, when I had a good day, when I had a bad day, when I wanted to go for a walk, talk, sing, or dance—they were there for me, not because they had nothing else going on, but because they cared. They even stuck up for me and spoke the truth when so many others seem to care only about image and what "good church going folk" would think. Thank you doesn't cut it. I owe so much of that peaceful feeling in my heart to them.

Even when our friends don't agree with our choices, they still support us on our path. Friends are able to celebrate differences. Who do you love inside out and backwards? Have you told them how you feel?

G

The very fact that you're reading this book means you're exploring new ways to go about your relationships—both the good and the not-so-good. If you don't already have a relationship with growing a *garden*, eating your *greens*, exuding *grace*, and honoring your *grandma*, then I recommend you revisit these priorities. There are a few relationships you may have, however, that I beg you to reconsider: *guilt* and *gluten*, both of which can wreak havoc on a compromised or unhealthy body.

GARDEN

Nature always has been a huge comfort to me, calming me and reminding me that like the lotus flower, I can handle anything that life's elements throw my way!

I always find something very primal and Paleo about eating something I have grown myself. It always tastes better, too. At my apartment, I don't have a garden because I am on the top floor. But I don't let that stop me from getting my hands dirty. I have herb plants on my patio, which overlooks the prettiest garden, a majestic weeping willow tree, a pond with a fountain, and countless Canadian geese. There are also flowers and super southern magnolia trees whose white flowers exude an intoxicating aroma that can stop me dead in my tracks.

When creating your garden, use organic potting soil to avoid those nasty chemicals in your bounty. If you don't have room to garden, start with just a basil plant. No space required, and who doesn't like a few fresh basil leaves on top of spaghetti or pizza? Or maybe you'd enjoy some fresh tomatoes, olive oil, and basil with a glass of red wine?

The sight of growing something, the smell of the earthy dirt, the taste of perky basil…a garden can awaken your senses and can bring you inner peace. Next time you desperately need to unplug from stress, stop and marvel at the ecosystem in your garden. The bees carry on while the butterflies flutter through their own flowery world of beauty. The green leaves and grasses reach and stretch toward the life-giving sun as if to beg for more warmth, more light, more life. Adapt these feelings to your current situation—you may be temporarily trapped in a life that has clipped your butterfly wings. Fear not! Even the caterpillar changed its life completely during its metamorphosis, and so can you. Do you think the little fuzzy guy knew what God had planned for him…or for you?

GLUTEN

Sales of gluten-free products have exploded recently, and even those who don't have a known wheat intolerance or Celiac disease are jumping on the gluten-free train. Gluten is a non-nutritive protein found in many nutritious grains that are rich in fiber, vitamins, and minerals. Bulgur, faro, kamut, and spelt are a few of these types of grains. Corn, potato, and rice are naturally gluten-free, but can be cross-contaminated if those grains are processed in factories where gluten products exist.

Much of our gluten intolerance these days has to do with how our plants are grown and processed in a GMO (genetically modified organism) society. Gluten proteins can have a way of, over time, attacking the lining of our intestines. The villi (think of a shag carpet) that move food through our digestive tract become weaker and can even begin to lie completely flat against the intestinal wall. This creates 20 plus feet of tract where food just hangs out all day, or month, or all year. The result is a perfect storm for bloating, gas, and indigestion, severe pain, allergies, leaky gut syndrome, excruciating pain, diarrhea, and constipation. Fun right?

In my experience, I have yet to see someone who has not benefited from reducing or eliminating gluten; weight loss and reduced bloating are much desired side effects. For many, gluten has to be completely avoided, but for most, it is a healthy subtraction to any well-rounded diet that includes plenty of protein and vegetables. If you're avoiding gluten, look for packages or products marked GLUTEN-FREE. Because gluten-free is big business and the products are more expensive, you have got to become a savvy shopper. All gluten-free products are not created equal. For example, there are countless gluten-free pancake mixes; many taste awful yet some taste really good. Experiment with different brands and see what you prefer. If losing a few pounds is your goal, it is best to eliminate as much as you can, which is very difficult because so many unsuspecting products contain gluten. Begin with the known gluten bombs: pasta, cookies, wheat products, chips, and breads. Read labels. Research online. Get to know what you're eating, how it's grown, and where it originates.

In general, reducing grains, whether gluten-free or not, is the way to go. They key is to eat very small portions of grains and fill up on fresh vegetables and lean proteins. Think about where your grains and simple carbohydrates are in your diet, and begin with one product that you consume every day. Switch it out for a gluten-free version. Things like cereal, waffles, toast, sandwich breads, and pastas are great places to start.

Take baby steps, Bella. Your immune system will be able to strengthen and restore nutrient absorption. By eliminating or reducing gluten, you are really loving yourself to health!

GRACE

Oh, the power of Grace. Essentially having grace is all about doing those things in life that we don't have to do, yet we put forth the effort anyway. Like if you are at a dinner party and your significant other asks you in a sweet voice if you would like another pour of a rare vintage wine. You graciously answer that you would love another sip to accompany the very last bite of your miso-glazed sea bass. As others around all have come to believe, you are absolutely the luckiest girl on the planet to be the recipient of such adoring, thoughtful attention. You secretly know that this kind person shows up for events but doesn't show up in your home. You, Bella, exemplify grace.

Grace always takes the high road. However, don't confuse Grace with being weak or a doormat. For me, there have been times when I scared the pants off of Grace and she hid behind the curtain because I piped up, spoke up, and was very unfiltered. *Yes, my name is Jeanine, and I am real woman with real feelings and can be pushed too far, and say exactly what I think!* Grace is strong because slow and steady wins the race. She is a quiet strength that builds more steadily as you allow her to show up in your life. Grace can be listening to a story 22 times that your toddler has told you, and every time you hear it, you say, "Oh my gosh! No way!" like it's the first time you've heard it. Grace can be the act of cutting some slack for a coworker who missed a deadline, but you know it's because she isn't feeling well these days. Let Grace show up in your life, and more often than not, she will smile upon you, just like the Grace of our Lord, who is always allowing us another chance…if we truly want one.

Philosophy®, the skin care company, sells a body spritz that is called Amazing Grace® and printed on the bottle is the coolest little reminder about how grace shows up in our life. It reminds us that how you go up is just as important as how you go down, and that life is one big gigantic lesson. Those lessons teach us to accept all of our being, the light and the dark. Not only will you smell nice but you will be reminded that there is a lesson for you somewhere in today.

GRANDMA

My grandmother, Grandma Carol, was born and raised in the Bronx by immigrant Italian parents, and she has had a considerable influence on my life. She is loving, feisty, strong, beautiful, dedicated to family, and knows the value of things like good health, hard work, saving for the future, being a good role model for children, and taking extra time to roll each meatball so it is perfectly round. Memories of my grandmother include snowy Christmas Eves when we would return from mass to a kitchen full of enough food and desserts to feed an army. Grandma Carol and my Grandpa split after my mom married, yet they remained friends and always respected each other. I can only imagine how difficult it must have been to make a relationship work when she got married at age 16.

My grandmother and I often talk on the phone. Before long, an hour will pass and we maybe touch on three different things. The fact is, is that when you love someone and you're enjoying your moments together, you really don't think about your own troubles. So during those conversations, I forgot about how hopeless I was feeling, and I escaped into a world where bonds aren't broken and love is given freely. After all, that is all love knows—how to give. Grandma Carol, you are the heart of this family, and therefore you live in all of our hearts.

Is there a matriarch—be it a grandmother, aunt, or other female influence—in your family with whom to celebrate a fountain of wisdom?

GREENS

Eat more greens! Eat your veggies! Most of us have heard this before. What if greens made you feel better and kept you healthier? What if they kept you regular and less bloated? What if they strengthen your bones more than milk ever could? What if they were a very important, irreplaceable brick in building the new you so that you become whole, healthy, and a little hotter after you detoxify from lunatics among you?

Dark leafy greens and broccoli are the biggest missing component in our diets today. We are all about silly big pieces of meat and potatoes, and yet green food is generally missing from our plates. Have you ever wondered why giraffes and elephants are so big and have the strongest bones? Did you know all they eat are leaves? Within those leaves are exactly the right doses of magnesium, calcium, iron, vitamin K2, and so many other vitamins and minerals that our nutritionally slaughtered diets do not provide. For those of you who tell me you don't like them, I call BS! What that tells me is you haven't *found or prepared* them a way you like them. Or it may mean that you eat too much sugar and salt, and then of course greens will be the last thing you crave. You have trained your taste buds to crave junk instead of real food. The shift doesn't happen overnight, but I will tell you that it can happen if you stay committed to healthy living.

I love my greens! I get so excited in Whole Foods Market® or the farmer's market when all of Mother Nature's bounty is spread out, colorful and so fresh. I must have some every day. Now, I don't love all of them and I would be lying if I said I did. Take beet greens for instance. I just can't stomach them, and that's okay. But I like kale, rainbow chard, spinach, lettuces, broccoli, and many more. Tough leaves like kale and chard are best in stews or heavily steamed. They can be very tough to digest raw, but they are great when you juice them! My point is, find something you like and it eat.

The fiber content in green veggies is huge, and although we associate fiber with a happy digestive system, its real role is to attach itself to things your body shouldn't have, such as viruses, bacteria, extra hormones like estrogen, and even protects us big time against cancer. So next time you want to do something good for yourself, make some steamed greens or a salad. Add nuts, seeds, boiled egg, or grilled salmon to it. You are keeping yourself strong during the storm, and laying the foundation for health and vitality. Trust me, the Big Bad Wolf may be smiling today, but tomorrow he's going to try to blow your house down, so be ready. Be strong!

GUILT

Guilt schmilt! Feeling guilty because your child said *shit* in his second grade class? Ok, you probably won't win Mother of the Year. Feeling guilty because you can't make your husband happy or you have to tell your children you are splitting up? This I understand entirely. However, that one is *not* your fault. Women in abusive relationships have to turn over every stone to save a dying marriage. Once you get to that point of no return— and only you can decide when that is—you will feel some degree of guilt. Not because you did anything wrong, but because you know your hands are tied, and that game of Jenga® will come tumbling down.

Now is a good time to shift your thinking about guilt. Will you feel guilty if your daughter sees you get spit on or disrespected by a man, and then accepts that as normal by a man later in life? It takes two to make it, but many times one to break it. I am not telling you that you will never feel guilty again, because I sometimes do. I also have learned that seeing my daughter for who she is and not who she is expected to be is a gift. Give your kids a barometer for healthy relationships. If it isn't the one you are in, begin your escape plan to get out. Walk the talk that love is kind, don't just preach it.

H

The entries under *H* really require you to consider thinking about some things in a new way. Perhaps you're frightened of what your future *holidays* will look like if you leave your current toxic situation. Or on the days when you feel low, how a good *haircut* can make the difference between you laughing or crying. Or how to *honor* yourself by *not* running into the arms of another man for comfort. What's your *hydration* situation? Are you drinking enough during your crazy days? Don't even get me started on *hydrocolon therapy*! My point is, sometimes in order to grow, we have to experience a little discomfort. But we don't have to sacrifice ourselves—or our hair!—in the process.

HAIR

Are you wondering how hair translates into health? I'm telling you, having your hair done is very cheap therapy! Do you know that feeling you get when you leave the salon a little more together than when you went in because you got a trim, a completely new style, highlights, or a color change? It's priceless. When my goddess of a stylist is done with my 'do, it is a great feeling to scoop up all the hair accessories I came in with and rock out the rest of my day in confidence. I usually have nowhere exciting to go on hair day, except school to get the kids, but hey, I go rockin' some shampooed *and* conditioned hair. That, Bella, is what made the day great.

The thing with hair is you can always change it. The truth is that feeling pretty is an inside and an outside thing. The confidence and security that we exude to others is sometimes boosted up by a great pair of shoes, a fantastic haircut, or a great workout. The same holds true when we feel depressed, fat, or hormonal.

Wearing that sexy bra or knock out pair of heels only adds to our irritability when we are not loving ourselves.

Because hair can be an important bridge to feeling a little lighter, pampered, and more together, make that appointment with your stylist. Don't have one? Ask around and find a new one. Let the stylist know what you are thinking about, and only get a style that you can maintain within the box of your lifestyle. Avoid drastic things that are going to require 30 minute blowouts in the morning if you have four kids to get to school by 7:30 a.m. Ask your stylist for techniques and tips on how he or she gets your hair so straight or frizz free. I've run the gamut between short and long hair, but I personally prefer to wear my hair long so I can put it in a bun during yoga, or wear it down, in a ponytail, or in a headband.

A nice and neat 'do isn't really vanity. I think it falls under the *general maintenance* category. You deserve to look and feel great, so make that appointment, get your hair washed, enjoy a scalp massage, and rock a new style, and let some of the ick in your life wash down the drain at the salon.

HAPPY HOUR

I am absolutely certain the first thing that comes to mind when you hear *happy hour* is a martini glass, wine glass, or even a Drambuie® on the rocks. Trust me, Bella, I'm with you. There's nothing like good friends, no judgment, chips and guacamole, laughter, a little black dress or maybe just flip flops and shorts. Location doesn't matter, either—a beach, a backyard, a driveway, or a kitchen table—you see, the *happy* can take place anywhere.

Now, let's reframe how we think of happy hour and make it something that does not sabotage waistlines and make our eyes puffy. The best thing about happy hour is generally spontaneous. For me, when I was having one of those super-challenging days where it seemed that the wrath from my relationship was coursing through my veins like radioactive green slime, I would get together with my best friends in the neighborhood, even if it was for 20 minutes. I already felt emotionally run over and I knew alcohol would have the ability to lift me up but then bring me down even further. So we would make Aloe-Tinis (see *Aloe*). Sometimes we would just have water with lots of lemon. It would be very easy to make excuses to drink alcohol, but I really wanted to *feel* good, and I knew that I had to make a shift in my happy hour technique.

Part of choosing to be whole, healthy, and a little bit hotter is to save the alcohol for when you really *want* it, and don't let it become a routine thing like brushing your teeth or going to work out. Your goal here is to have more energy and sleep better so that you can handle all the crap coming your way and feel alive. Don't deaden your senses with constant alcohol. Get together with friends, enjoy the camaraderie, and celebrate life. I love to meet my friends and go for walks or maybe get a green juice smoothie. Alcohol-free soirees are great for your weight and your ticker! Repeat after me: *I can visit with my friends and not have to involve alcohol or food. Salud!*

HOLIDAYS

Once you realize your family is not forever and you are going to leave a relationship, or have just left it, the fallout can wreak havoc on your holidays if you let it. This new space will be a prison if you allow it to be. What I realized, and you will too, is that nothing can take away holiday joy because if you are celebrating these holidays with any resemblance of the true spirit, then it lives inside of you and *is not up for grabs.*

Holidays for me are a time of celebrating faith, family, friends, and much anticipated time off from work or school. I feel such a high when I buy gifts for those I love. I love the music, the traditions, the food, and the memories I make. That's the part that can make me feel so elated. But there's always the potential to become deeply depressed—the worst for me is holiday time without my kids. I mourn the departure from my old house and the memories within—laughing, children, cooking turkeys, decorating Christmas trees, setting tables elegantly with candles and crystal, snuggling on the couch with my kids, and watching twinkling tree lights. This is where reframing how I think about the holidays saves me from the slump.

Now, I will get a much smaller tree, I will replace decorations that I lost during my divorce, I will put on my Christmas music and dance, I will watch the flurries from my new balcony, I will cook my favorite cookies and stews, and I will celebrate the reason for the season. I will see my son when he comes home from college, I will visit with friends, I will spend as much time with my daughter as possible, and I will be grateful that I have what I have. I will get down on my knees and thank Jesus for giving me the strength to move through this ordeal, and for the new gifts He has so gracefully bestowed upon me, all while never giving up on me that I will continue hear His messages that are like whispers to my heart.

My dear Bella, I wish I could give you a hug at this moment. I want you to know that I have experienced that misery that you feel in your heart. That terrifyingly painful ache is what immobilizes you and keeps you standing in that very spot because the pain of leaving is just too much to bear. This is why you must recognize it, and place your hand over your heart and tell yourself that *you love you.* You must realize that you no longer have to be doomed to life where you are the supporting actress in someone else's movie. You have everything you need anyway because chances are that while you are decorating your home or even at church on Christmas Eve, your significant other is mostly likely on a date, planning a date, or just left a date. Let me hear a big *Hell no!* if that junk can be thrown out with last year's Christmas tree!

You no longer have to live to make someone else look good. You don't have to bear the burden to protect anyone anymore.

Acknowledge that you love yourself so much, and but for a few shifts in your holidays as you have come to know them, you are allowing more love to flow into your life, and into your children's lives. Open your heart to feeling and knowing the truth, and know that around the corner lies another tree waiting to be lit, another kitchen stove waiting to become the heart of your home, and another couch for you to snuggle and watch *Frosty the Snowman* with your kids.

You gave him too much of your past. Don't give him your future. Give your children new memories of simple joy and a mother who knows how to protect what is undeniably the God-given right of human dignity. What is certain in an uncertain world is that staying where you are will continue to kill your spirit, and could eventually kill you.

HOME

I think your *home* is different from your *nest* and here's why. Home is a feeling, in addition to being a place. Home is that spot where you belong just because you're you. Home is the people who embrace you completely every time you're there.

For me, it's my parents' house in New York. When I am home, my heart and body can truly rest. Despite any difficulty in my life, or my kids' lives, every last challenge seems to melt away when I'm there because I'm enchanted by the unconditional love that resides under that roof. I sleep so soundly when I'm in my old bedroom at my parent's house. There are trinkets that still hold the memories of long ago, along with the rows of embarrassing old photographs that depict my not-so-cool hairstyles. The air even smells different there. The true magic is that when I am visiting in New York, I immediately and completely transform back into that young girl I used to be—daring, confident, and ready to tackle the world.

Is it always easy to make these moments happen? No, not always. Sometimes you have to get by with just an extra long phone call with someone who is home when you can't be. Money can't buy happiness, but it can buy your airline ticket or a tank of gas. Because hugs and being home are big priorities for me, I often forgo purchasing extra items if it means that I can buy airlines tickets home instead. Whether you find out that your spouse has a big date planned *because* you are out of town, or you're stressed about beginning a new job, the realities of what is important to you will begin to bubble to the surface once you reconnect with home. Even your kids may morph into a different vibe because they never even knew how much they needed a shift in gears until they got there.

Forget your troubles, even for a few moments, and go home— physically or mentally. Take out that old photo album, call a loved one, or tonight for dinner serve something the way your grandfather used to make it. Connect to yourself and your roots for that validation you crave. Show your children that home is a legacy of comfort, unconditional love, and acceptance.

HONOR

Acting with honor adds to this book's message about coming out of your fiasco whole. I am the first one to admit that it isn't always easy, but then again, nothing worth having ever is. Many of you are dealing with a cheating spouse. Let's just suppose your significant other frequently travels down the path that leads to someone else's bed, shower, car, or gym. Once you learn of these indiscretions, you may feel like someone has punched you in the gut. Suppose that he continues to see this other person, or other people? Suppose this continues for years or decades? How easy would it be for you to find solace in the arms of a gorgeous, virile, affectionate man who says all the things you should be hearing from your spouse? It is way too easy to go down that road—and what of the emotional and mental price you pay afterward?

This is where honor comes in. Traditional wedding vows usually include words like, *I promise to love, cherish, and honor until death do us part*. Last I checked, there was no clause saying, *only if you do*. So here, Bella, lies the honor part. You are to be cherished, and you may be the only one who can do it. You know you will never get blood from a stone, so quit looking to the one who causes you pain to take it away. Although your moment of validation in the sexy, strong, masculine arms of a stranger gives your femininity and ego a boost and reminds you that you are living, breathing woman, the tradeoff is a tiny sliver of your honor that cannot be replaced...*ever*. And if you are not careful, any alimony due to you may be up for grabs, too. You stayed honorable for so long, why change now? This too shall pass, and you will be more whole for the experience. Then, when *you* decide it's the right time, he will be one lucky man!

HYDRATION

One of the biggest yet basic challenges I see clients struggling with is staying properly hydrated. It really can be a simple fix for what ails you.

But did you know that replacing electrolytes is also an important part of hydration? Electrolytes are minerals like sodium, chloride, calcium, potassium, magnesium whose job is to regulate where fluids are distributed in the body. They are positively and negatively charged particles that are formed when minerals, such as salts, dissolve in water. They can conduct an electrical current in the water to regulate hydration, which is why they are vitally important. We know that excessive sodium can raise our blood pressure, and often times lowering dietary sodium may not necessarily lower blood pressure. Sometimes regulating all of the electrolytes is what can help normalize blood pressure. It is likely that potassium levels actually need to be raised.

Coconut water is a fantastic example of a healthy electrolyte drink, and actually packs a potassium punch far greater than a banana. It contains some natural sugar, so even diluting coconut water with plain water can be a great post-workout drink. I love a product called Ultima Replenisher® (www.ultimareplenisher.com), which is a balanced electrolyte powder that contains no artificial ingredients and is sweetened with stevia powder. It isn't overloaded with mega doses of electrolytes, and it replaces what is lost during exercise. My favorite flavors are grape and orange, and I drink it throughout the day. It dissolves pretty quickly in room temperature water, but because stevia is more fiber-like than sugar, it may require a little stir or shake. In a society that supports sporting your own re-usable water bottles, make sure that you have plenty to drink throughout the day. Ultima® will help keep those sweet cravings at bay, too. (For those of you who have children, it's best not to give them sugary and artificially-flavored sports drinks. Teach their taste buds right from the start, and they won't ever have to detox from mainstream sports drinks.)

You are running in the most intense sprint of your life. You just don't realize it. Your body is working so hard to maintain its health in a toxic mental environment. Staying properly hydrated will help you sleep better, flush out toxins, and avoid headaches.

HYDROCOLON THERAPY

I realize that there are three types of people when it comes to this topic: (1) those who have never heard of it before; (2) those who have heard of it and give it a big *hell no!;* and (3) those who have done it. The third group is by far the smallest one. There is so much conflicting information and opinions about hydrocolonics—sometimes known as enemas or colon irrigation—and rightfully so. It seems that within all things health or prevention, this is just the nature of the beast.

I'll let you in on a secret. I've done it. I do it once or twice a year. I plan on always doing it. I feel like a million bucks when I do it. I have only the best therapist around. I always take probiotics, especially following a hydrocolonic, to build intestinal flora. I believe we need it because we commit nutritional slaughter and live highly toxic lives. I believe that in a perfect world, we would not need it because our body is designed to run efficiently; however, chips, soda, wine, artificial sweeteners, low-fiber diets, chocolate brownies, milk, sugar, Skittles, too much meat and cheese, processed cereals, and low-quality vitamins ingested for a few decades surely messes with our 20 feet of small intestine and five feet of large intestine.

It's a personal choice and one that you must research. Many health and wellness spas offer a colonic as part of a detox ritual. They're more common than you think. I always do it after a month-long detox of no alcohol, caffeine, dairy, gluten, and sugar. Find someone in your area and ask questions. Or visit my therapist's FAQ page at www.intestinalfitnessllc.com/faq.html to get answers to all the things you are dying to know but too embarrassed to ask. It is not as weird or embarrassing as you may think! Is it time to consider a colonic? Get rid of years of undigested...um...stuff with a series of three sessions. Your body will absorb nutrients and detox so much better. I shit you not!

I

I is mostly about introspection and self-worth. *Identity, image, inner child,* and *intuition* all ask you to delve a little deeper into who you are, why you're where you are, and who you want to become. *Ingredients*, which nourish your body as well as your soul, are mostly about self-health. Remember, garbage in, garbage out.

IDENTITY

Labels are everywhere—on our clothes, cars, computers, phones. We even label ourselves—sales manager, president, executive, bitch, divorcee, single, loser, team leader, smoker, hipster, single mom, ADHD. It seems our identity is wrapped up is these very labels that we place (literally and figuratively) on ourselves and on others. Here's some truth: Your identity is really not attached to any of these ideas at all.

Don't misunderstand me here. I appreciate many of the finer things in life. My point is that we are neither *more* if we have them, nor *less* if we don't. I am the same person when I sit in first class as I am when I sit in coach, just with less of a back ache!

Imagine right now Category 5 hurricane rips through your town and whisks away your house and with it your BMW, your *Christian Louboutin* shoes, your David Yurman jewelry, your cheap coffee pot, your $3 flip flops, and your Old Navy® tank tops. You are surrounded by miles of debris that was once your home and belongings. Post-storm, no one is able to tell that you make $1.5 million a year because your belongings are enmeshed with those of the bus driver who makes $21 grand a year driving your children to school. There you both sit in disbelief as you recoil from the horror of what just happened. You just feel beyond grateful to be alive. The Category 5 will never be able to take away your identity.

Neither will this toxic relationship. Ask yourself this: Who am I? What do I believe? Do my outward actions align with my inner beliefs? If you can't answer these questions, start today by doing small things to rebuild a new life without judgment for others…or yourself. Your identity is something to salvage from the wreckage around you.

IMAGE

This ties in nicely with *Identity*. Image is what you put out there so people see you how you want to be seen (happily married, well-behaved children, successful, all-American family). Integrity is how God sees you (fulfilled, imperfectly perfect, emotionally void, kind, selfish). Do your guts match your glory? If they don't right now, then work toward having them mesh. No one is perfect or has the perfect life. No one. Trying to live more authentically with integrity means a win-win for everyone in the end.

INGREDIENTS

In a busy and hectic life, sometimes less is more. Take ingredients for example. It seems to me that the best comfort foods and even the healthiest dishes call for only a few simple yet fresh items. Sometimes life calls for quick, right? Anyone who has work and children demands knows that life doesn't always allow time to slice, dice, sauté, and bake. Here are a few of my go-tos for when life is tugging at me:

- Iceberg lettuce with sliced avocado and turkey.

- Rotisserie chicken from Whole Foods Market® with a side of steamed broccoli.

- Hillary's® frozen veggie burgers (soy-, gluten-, dairy-, and nut-free) with a side salad.

- Rao's® tomato sauce with gluten-free angel hair pasta, parsley, and basil and a side of any veggie or salad.

- So Delicious® dairy-free *plain* coconut milk yogurt with raspberries and slivered almonds.

- Unsweetened almond milk (or rice, hemp, or flax) with Vega® smoothie mix.

- Dr. Oetker® frozen pizza topped with extra veggies and a spinach salad on the side.

- Steamed cauliflower, mashed with chicken broth, salt, and pepper.

- Veggie omelets with organic eggs (who doesn't love breakfast for dinner?).

- Celery with almond butter (a much healthier option than peanut butter).

My Italian roots beg me to add more, but this would wind up being a cookbook! When was the last time you cooked something simple but delicious? Experiment and find something new to try. Keep staples in your pantry—I like parsley, olive oil, salt, pepper, and garlic—so you're not rushing around when it's crunch time. Visit your local organic grocery store or shop in the natural section of your local store for ideas. Give yourself 10 extra minutes to peruse the produce and read package labels.

A few words of caution: you can't feel like a million bucks if you eat off the dollar menu! Overprocessed prepared meals and non-food substances like high fructose corn syrup, transfats, artificial sweeteners like sucralose (Splenda®) or *aspartame (Equal®),* or any artificial colors like Yellow #5, Red #40, and Blue #1, have no business in your pantry. Staying committed to your future means that you need to choose what you want *most* in life, not what you want *now*!

INNER CHILD

When did you become so serious? Was it when you realized you were really in a difficult and toxic relationship and *someone* needed to be the grown-up? When was the last time you jumped on a trampoline or climbed a tree? Has it been decades since you sang out loud and off-key to your favorite song? When was the last time you caught fireflies in a jar or watched a Pixar movie with your child? Have you ever run through a corn maze with your kids in the crisp autumn air? Or smeared whipped cream or cake frosting on a friend's forehead just for giggles?

I often turned my back on my inner child. One year, though, I took her to Disney World. A pack of friends and their children, and my daughter Lily and I high-tailed it to Orlando for laughs, fun, rides, and great wines and food. The apex was being with my dear friends for four days. I found myself singing and skipping and loving all that our trip had to offer. My inner child was alive and vibrant.

It was on that trip that my friend gave me a glittery snow globe that plays "A Dream Is a Wish Your Heart Makes." When I hear that song my inner child springs from her hibernation and I am seven years old again. The song has the power to take me far away from whatever crisis I'm contending with. How's this for an affirmation? *I AM NOT USELESS. I AM A BEAUTIFUL PRINCESS AND DESERVE TO BE TREATED WITH RESPECT.*

Things like climbing trees, walking barefoot, swinging on a tire, going down a slide, watching *Tom and Jerry*, skipping, and even eating olives off your fingers all have a place in your healing. Your inner child is there to remind you of who you are. If you can't take her to Disney, take her to the playground or for heaven's sake, let her lick the cake batter spoon. She needs you.

INTUITION

In-tu-i-tion/in-too-ish-uh | n/noun: the ability to understand something immediately without the need for conscience reasoning.

Navigating the waters of intuition without a physical compass can be treacherous. Once your gut pings you that something just isn't quite right, you may begin to feel that everything isn't quite right. You may feel that he wasn't at the gym when he said he was, so he's probably not at the office when he says he is. You can drive yourself mad! It wasn't until I started changing my prayers that my intuition (I like to think of it as God's message) spoke louder to me: *Dear Lord, please strengthen me and show me the way. I am a big girl and can handle the truth. Show me truth and help me to recognize reality when I come across it.*

Every day, and not only in relationships, ask for the truth to be revealed to you. Make no mistake about it, *when it is time* for you to be in the know, you will know. It can be frustrating because you may be used to setting your own time limits and to expecting things to shift just because you say they should. Wrong! This is a time to trust in your intuition. That's the tough part. You see, there is a much larger, all-knowing force that whispers to you: *All in good time my dear, all in good time.* This spiritual awakening is deeply humbling and grounding.

Clarity through intuition will not be the proverbial piano dropped on your head, but the message and transparency it brings with it will be just as colossal. The right people will *just happen* to cross your path. Old friends will know something of interest or information you need will become accessible. Someone will *accidentally* share something with you. All sorts of puzzle pieces will come together, and your intuition will allow you to be in the right spot at the right time. That little voice will nudge you to skip the grocery store and go straight home even though you don't have anything planned for dinner! Stay open, focused, pray for truth, and spend at least 10 quiet minutes a day clearing your brain from what you *think* is true, and making room in your thoughts for what is *actually* true.

You must continue to keep an open mind and an open heart once God has decided that your attention is finally focused. Now is the time to continue to ask for guidance. Don't dismiss that little voice inside because it carries with it the necessary ingredients in your recipe of life. Blessings are all around you. They may be wrapped up in an extra long hug from your child or maybe there is just an air of peace and tranquility in the home tonight.

Be forewarned: buckle up for safety because the ride can get scary, if not downright terrifying. Listening to your intuition takes practice, as does being patient and staying open to hearing the truth. By staying healthy physically and mentally, you're preparing yourself to act on the truths you learn.

J

Continuing on the path of self-introspection, I present to you the letter *J*. Get to know yourself better by starting a *journal* of your daily happenings. I find knowing *Jesus* to be a tremendous comfort and spiritually renewing. *Jeanine* thought long and hard about the beautiful spirit she is and realized her own potential, likes, and dislikes—just as you will discover who you really are and what you're all about! It's not exactly self-introspective, but it is self-healthy...*juicing* is a refreshing way to take charge of your health and energy. Give it a try!

JEANINE

She was a baby who rarely slept and hardly cried, a curious toddler who tried to keep up with her older sisters and played outside barefoot, and a pre-teen who just tried to blend in. She was a teenager who loved to travel and fell in love with a good man. She became a young woman who married and gave birth to a ridiculously awesome son. Then she became a divorced working mother—one who was not so perfect but always tried to do what was right. She then was a remarried woman who had a beautiful baby girl and a toxic marriage. Finally, she was a woman who began to shed all of the ideas about who she thought she was supposed to be.

Jeanine is now back to being the same person who grew up in that loving Italian family, and she is creating those same traditions and boundaries so her own children can someday travel the world yet still know where *home* really is. She is imperfectly perfect. She is content in her likes and dislikes: She loves eating veggies, almond butter, and ice cream, listening to love songs, watching funny movies, breathing crisp autumn air, drinking wine, being held by strong masculine arms, feeling butterflies in her stomach, seeing angels, practicing yoga, being a health coach, wearing flip flops, dancing slowly, hearing her son's voice, sniffing her daughters head, and inspiring health in others. She doesn't like someone prepping her coffee, people who are self-serving, rude kids, wasps and hornets, capers, PMS, men who act immature, movies about girls or women being abused, pushy people, beer, or amalgam dental fillings. She will continue to evolve and embrace her gray hair and wrinkles. She knows she will be and feel more beautiful than ever a she ages with grace and fortitude. I like Jeanine, and so do *those who matter*.

Write a paragraph about yourself. Who were you then and who are you now? Do you embrace your likes and dislikes? This is an essential exercise in self-discovery. No matter what you decide to write, remember that you are a beautiful spirit. This activity is a step toward vacating the space you feel trapped in, and will help you get to know yourself again. You aren't perfect—nobody is—and that's perfectly okay.

JESUS

It's difficult to capture in mere, mortal words the magnitude of strength I have gotten from my relationship with Jesus.

I'm not preaching here. I'm just sharing my awe: If Jesus could be vilely abused in the ways in which He had been and yet still possess unwavering faith in His Holy Father and compassion for mankind in all their wrongdoings, then I can continue to find ways to manage the ill intentions from those who don't love and support me. In the dark corners of my being where such grotesque robbery played out time and time again, there is a flicker of light that no person will ever be able to dampen. The one who ignites that light is Jesus, the coolest, most loving and forgiving guy I know.

JOURNAL

If you don't know where you have been, how do you know where you are going? By journaling you can discover all sorts of neat tidbits about yourself. Keeping a journal is a powerful tool that is helpful when trying to create new, positive habits. It can force you realize that you only had 20 ounces of water all day when you are really shooting for 80 ounces. Or that you had seven cookies, not three. Think you exercised three days this week? You might flip back through the pages of your journal and realize that you actually did four! Gotta love a win! My advice with journaling is this: Don't share it with others. It contains your private thoughts.

I know how difficult it can be to write down things that you'd rather forget, ignore, or let fade from memory, such as the day you were short with your child because the asparagus you asked her to try sent her into a tantrum. Or maybe you'd like to forget the day that you wanted to have just one piece of pizza, but your hoodlum hormones won out and you had three. Writing things down makes us feel vulnerable, yet can keep us accountable to ourselves. Don't lie to yourself.

Once you know where your roadblocks are you can begin to remove them, but you won't know them unless you're truthful with yourself. The truth sucks at first, but then it sets you free. As the person who holds your family together, you probably have a tendency to overlook the personal assaults because you become numb to them. Things like mean-spirited words, neglect, deceit, and other forms of abuse are exactly the things you should be putting in your journal. By journaling your events, you will never forget, but more importantly, you will be able to see trends that are difficult to see while you are up to your eyeballs in life's murky waters. It is like that old saying, *You can't see the forest for the trees*. Well, Bella, unless you're writing these things down, you'll stay lost in the woods.

Never kept a journal before? Start today by getting a journal or by creating a password-protected document—anything will do, just get your thoughts down in writing. You'll change your perspective and make better decisions based on not only your feelings, but also on the facts and truths within the pages. Write them down, make them real, and do something today your future self will thank you for.

JUICING

Juicing can be a nourishing component to a healthy lifestyle—if you juice the right foods. When you juice, you are removing all of the fiber from the fruits and veggies. When you remove fiber the resulting liquid does not have to travel through your digestive system for absorption and elimination. The nutrients are bioavailable and absorb immediately beginning in your mouth. On the other hand, when you make a smoothie from fruits and veggies in your blender, it contains all of the fiber and must be digested.

Juicing can be part of a short-term detox, but should never be considered a meal replacement because it lacks protein, fiber, and fat—the macronutrients needed to function properly. And be forewarned: juicing apples, pineapples, and carrots may taste great, but if you drink a 10-ounce glass, you are drinking as much sugar as in a can of soda (about 40 grams)! If I'm going to have that much sugar at once, it is going to be from a chocolate soufflé. Sugar is sugar is sugar.

If you don't want to gain weight and spike your insulin from your healthy juice, then add more veggies. Try cucumber, celery, parsley, and maybe add a slice of apple, pineapple, or even a carrot for a little sweetness. Celery and cucumbers have high water content so they make a pretty large glass. The only rule is don't derail your health with sugar-filled juices. In fact, I advise everyone to cut out juice unless you make it yourself with mostly veggies. You can have your juice and drink it, too!

K

There are only two points I touch on in this brief section. In keeping with my philosophy of eating greens daily, here I espouse the benefits of *kale*. *Karma* is one concept that many of us have heard of, but may not have really considered in the grand scheme of our lives. Take a moment in this section to consider how Karma has acted out in your life. The answers you find may surprise you.

KALE

Let me try on my best Bubba Gump impression: *You've got your steamed kale, your sautéed kale, your Tuscan kale soup, your baked kale chips, your roasted kale, your raw kale, your kale smoothie and so on.* Kale is a movie star these days with its versatility becoming renowned. Two decades ago, if you got a curly, tough, ugly green leaf under your chicken breast sandwich at a chain restaurant, you probably had no idea what it was. You certainly didn't entertain the thought of eating it.

Kale is the mother of all calcium and it is a cruciferous vegetable related to broccoli and cauliflower. It is always a player on any top 10 list of healthiest foods. It's loaded with fiber, calcium, vitamin C, and beta carotene. The leaves have a nice, mild flavor and there are many ways to prepare it (see above endorsements). Always wash thoroughly before using—try using a salad spinner to get all remaining wetness off of the leaves when using kale in a salad. You can cut out the tough, fibrous middle stalk and chop it for a sauté or throw it into your juicer. When cooked, it becomes a beautiful bright green. Or try it raw as a ceviche-style dish by adding fresh-squeezed lemon or lime juice and a pinch of salt. As it marinates, the acid in the citrus softens the leaves, leaving it easier to digest.

I recommend that you prepare kale however you enjoy it most. However, consider that the less a food is cooked, the more nutrients it has. I buy bags of frozen kale, or freeze my own, and then add a handful to my breakfast smoothie that I zap in my NutriBullet® blender. It's a healthy and simple way to get those greens in daily. Just make sure you have dental floss on hand because that kale has way of getting stuck in your teeth! With so many varieties to choose from, adding kale into your diet will fortify your bones, help your immune system, and support the detoxification and elimination process. Kale is really what does a body good.

KARMA

It's a little difficult to sum up Karma briefly, but it's the basic concept of *what comes around goes around*. As much as we like the "goes around" part, some of us conveniently subtract ourselves from the "comes around" part of the equation. I have seen Karma play out in my own life, and I have joyfully been on the watching side and humbly been on the receiving side. We all have—that's how life works. At some point, though, we have to learn lessons when situations "come around" to us. I believe that it happens only when God feels that the timing is right. Who doesn't want to see someone get their payback for all of the ways they have hurt us? Maybe you've even imagined the many ways your toxic partner gets his, the whole time wishing you could be there to bear witness.

These are all very natural feelings to have. All you can do is have faith that they will learn their lesson. Chances are, though, that you may not have front-row tickets when it all goes down. It may happen 20 years later and you may never ever know about it. Karma acts in the universe's timing, not ours. So, next time you get to imagining that the Karma fairy will show up with those front-row tickets, rest assured that Karma *will* be fulfilled. It just might unfold when the movie theater has closed and everyone's gone home for the evening. The Divine Spirit will be watching. Let it go, and let Karma unfold in its own time. We know not what the big picture is.

L

The overarching theme of L is *learning*: learning to read *labels* to educate yourself about what's in the food you eat. Learning to appreciate a change of scenery with a *latitude adjustment*. Learning to find your *laughter* and appreciate how much better you feel when you do. Learning to love *lemons* in all their sour glory. Learning to *learn* about yourself and what you still have to learn. And finally, learning to *let go*—of headache, heartache, and everything in between.

LABELS

I can't stress enough the importance of reading the labels on your food items. And not just the *all natural* or *new and improved* labels. I'm talking about the nutritional content box that lists calories, fat grams, carbs, and most importantly, ingredients! Does your apple, wild salmon, or broccoli come with a label? Heavens no. The healthiest foods are minimally processed and have no labels. Consider that food is information. It tells you how to feel, sleep, manage hormones, and can help give you mental clarity. If you fill up your tank with junk, it will be full (briefly) but your engine will not run for long and it will eventually break down. Toxic, chemicalized junk ingredients are quick-burn "fuel" and won't nourish your body and won't help it run efficiently. If you want to exponentially increase your odds of having vibrant future life, quit committing nutritional slaughter to your beautiful parts!

The following chemical labels are nonfood substances created in a lab, not by Mother Nature, and have no place in your diet:

- **Partially hydrogenated oils (transfats):** Raise your LDL (bad) cholesterol and are attributed to coronary heart disease. Transfats are found in many shelf-stable foods such as breads, sauces, cookies, cakes, coffee creamer, candy, dressings, chips, etc.

- **High fructose corn syrup (HFCS):** Despite the billion-dollar marketing campaign that tells you it is just like sugar, it's not. HFCS is an industrially produced sweetener found in most poor-quality and nutrient-deficient products. It is cheap for food manufacturers to use, thus products with HFCS are cheaper and sweeter than products with cane sugar. HFCS taxes the liver, drives up cholesterol, turns off the body's ability to tell you that you are full, and adds to our catastrophic proportions of obesity.

- **Artificial colors:** Yellow #5, Red #40, and Blue #1 and other artificial colors are created in a lab and have been linked to everything from cancer to ADHD.

- **Artificial sweeteners:** Those pretty pink, blue, and yellow packets might as well have a skull and crossbones on them. Most of these are also created in a lab. Did you know the saccharin was accidentally discovered while scientists were working on coal tar derivatives? Yuck!

Suffice it to say, by reading the labels of what you consume, you're educating yourself and empowering yourself to be in charge of what you put into your body. And your body will thank you for it by having more energy, fewer illnesses, and an overall healthy feeling.

LATITUDE ADJUSTMENT

A dear friend of mine coined the phrase *Latitude Adjustment*, and Jimmy Buffet sang of changes in latitude. I think they're onto something. One should never, ever under estimate the power of a change in latitude. I have enjoyed travel from when I was a little girl. When I was 19 years old, I became a travel agent and I absolutely loved it. I researched and planned my clients' trips with scrupulous detail, and even more so when those trips were mine! From Tahiti to Europe to South America, I have been blessed to stay in some of the nicest resorts, dine at the most spectacular restaurants, drink some of the rarest wines, and feel as though history was happening all around me. Even after I had children, I loved whisking them away, even if it was just for the day. I guess you could say I was a latitude adjustment junkie.

The best parts of traveling are the forever memories that no person can steal from you. At this point in my life, I would rather be on the beach in North Carolina near my home with someone who cares about my thoughts than be in the presidential suite in Las Vegas with someone who doesn't.

When was the last time you got away? Was it alone? Was it with the good mood vampire? Was it with fun people? Plan a latitude adjustment. It doesn't have to be costly. It could be a drive to the coast or to the mountains for the day. It could be going to visit that friend who moved three years ago and keeps begging you to see her. Stop denying yourself pleasure of every kind, and adjust your attitude with a latitude shift. Farm out the kids or bring them with you. Just book it. As with most things, the world will not blow up and you will come back more whole than when you left. You don't even have to take pictures. It'll be your moment to savor. Your secret is safe with me.

LAUGHTER

I once presented at a women's health workshop where we discussed the secrets of the centenarians—that's the worldwide community of people thriving past the ripe young age of 100. Dan Buettner discusses in his book *The Blue Zones* the secrets of longevity and the connection to happiness and laughter. He talks about how there are the most people aged 100 or older than 100 thriving in five areas: Costa Rica's isolated Nicoya

Peninsula, Sardinia, Ikaria—a remote Greek Island, Okinawa, and a small community in southern California named Loma Linda. I find it fascinating that some of the communities drink wine, and others don't. Some eat fish, others are vegetarian. There are other differences, but what is similar between all of them is they eat zero processed food and they maintain social relationships that provide laughter and joy.

Think about it. We always hear laughter is the best medicine. Why is that? Both humor and laughter can make you feel good. Humor is a handy communication tool to relieve tension between people and to facilitate relationship-building. It also helps us cope with emotions such as sadness, fear, grief, and anger. The hormones adrenaline and cortisol are released to help us manage stress are counteracted by serotonin—the happy hormone—which in turn relaxes us and has the power to change our thoughts completely. Laughter is often thought of as common sense medicine. Makes perfect sense to me!

Choose to spend your precious time around people who lift your up spirits, not bring them down. For instance, my son is the funniest person I know. I always feel better after he calls, no matter what is going on with my day. We both laugh so hard at the silliest things until our stomachs hurts. My daughter is also so clever and funny that sometimes I can't believe that we can carry on as often as we do. We dance, we sing, we laugh, we love, and we go through this life together enmeshed in ways that are stronger than steel. My friends and my sisters also keep my serotonin supply topped off.

I promise you that amidst all of the struggles and obstacles that you feel are crushing down on you, your laughter is a glimmer of hope. It is your inner child wanting to come out to play. Laughter is a necessary component to living a long a fruitful life. Don't forget to laugh at yourself when you're being silly because from your tiny chuckles of *Who are you and what did you do with me?* come yet another source of fortitude for your new, happier, more beautiful and healthy self.

LEARN

You'll probably never learn more about yourself or how life can turn on a dime than you will during your time during or after a toxic relationship. Life is full of those moments when you learn so much about yourself and how you feel in different situations.

When you had youth on your side and you weren't wired to feel the slightest bit of mortality, you probably made downright stupid decisions. Like those times in college when you stayed out until 2:00 a.m. drinking when you had a class at 8:00 a.m. Even as a seasoned adult, you can sometimes make not-so-super decisions. Like the time you allowed someone access to your deepest and darkest thoughts, and they turned their back on you, judging you as they walked away while conveniently forgetting their own faults and vulnerabilities.

Now you don't have the luxury of youthful folly or bad decision-making on which to blame your mistakes. Surviving this relationship requires strength and self-awareness. You will learn you are forever a student, and you will come to realize that keeping an open mind is just as important as keeping an open heart. You can learn from watching your own parents, from listening to your friends or colleagues, or from listening to that little gut feeling in the pit of your stomach. Learning can be factual, emotional, or spiritual. As you open more and more, just like the strong and beautiful lotus flower, you will flourish into a new you with each new thing you learn.

Along my journey of self-discovery, I learned more about divorce and child custody laws than I ever thought possible. It wasn't always positive, but by knowing the laws and how to best navigate the stormy seas of litigation and separation, I was able to create the best *possible* scenario for my future. In reality, right doesn't always win, and justice doesn't always prevail. I read, researched, and advocated for myself and my children. My close friends and family were a GPS for me, always informing me and directing me toward my goals. I learned from their experience and knowledge base.

When you are caught up in a web of deception and nothing makes sense, your own reality can become distorted. Learn to stay present. Learn to keep an open mind. Learn to rely on the trustworthy angels you call friends. Learn to trust your intuition. And learn that you have so much yet to learn.

LEMONS

Lemons are a low-calorie, low-sugar, antioxidant-rich addition to most diets. Many people associate lemons with acid and reflux, but the opposite is true. The citric acid in lemons (and limes), once inside the body, actually neutralizes acid production and creates a more alkalized pH level inside the body. I have seen time and time again that when people who experience reflux add lemon water to their diet, they see a marked reduction in their symptoms. It is always helpful to reduce coffee, alcohol, and smoking if symptoms are severe. By drinking 8–10 ounces of water with the juice of half a lemon first thing in the morning, you lower your body's pH and activate your liver for the day. Your liver is like the air filter in your home. If you never change it, the air gets stale, carpets get dirty, and you breathe in all sorts of pollen, dander, and dust mites. That is disgusting! It's sort of the same with your liver. If you don't give it a little scrub every day, the overall health of your body can begin to decline.

Lemons are incredibly versatile. Besides adding to your water, you can squeeze a lemon into fresh veggie juices, chicken stock, salad dressing, or even over fish. Don't forget about Meyer lemons! They are scrumptious and can be eaten raw— peel and all. Next time you are at the store, pick up a few lemons and limes and keep them on your counter so you remember to use them. Now for the gusto part—when life hands you lemons, it's okay to make *limoncello*. *Salud!*

LET GO

Letting go and not clinging to things or people who no longer serve us is one tough challenge. Why is it that so many of us need to bang our heads against the wall before we get the message? Is it because our intentions are pure, honest, and benevolent for all? Or maybe it's because we have a glass half-full way of looking at things? Is it because we feel if we could do more, give more, love more, and bend more everything would be okay?

Regardless of the reasons, we sometimes have extreme difficulty letting go of things that aren't good for us. That is how we wind up compromising our happiness and self-worth. Don't confuse letting go with giving up. They are not the same. Letting go is giving ourselves permission to clean house and get rid of the emotional clutter that's gumming up our clarity and preventing us from achieving inner happiness. Isn't it time to self-preserve and let go?

The leaves fall in autumn because if they didn't, the weight of the snow would pile on the leaves to tear down the braches. Your branches are about to break, so shed your leaves and hunker down. Spring is just around the corner and with it brings a vibrant season of renewal and new life. Don't you want in on that? Let go and let God. Do what you can, and allow the Divine Spirit to handle the big picture. Keep in mind the following prayer:

God grant me

the serenity to accept the things I cannot change,

the courage to change the things I can,

and the wisdom to know the difference.

M

M is for maintaining your body, mind, and well-being. Learn more about *magnesium*, the super-mineral that is like a little personal trainer for your body in how it helps your muscles and your, well...everything! Revisit how and why you wear *makeup*, and how you feel when you listen to your favorite *music*. When you *meditate* you practice the ancient art of getting in touch with your innermost thoughts and center yourself for the day. When you hear *mom*, do you think of synonyms like love, comfort, security, and warm hugs? Think about the feelings that are evoked when you spend *money*. Finally, you just may reconsider sleeping in when you think about all the wonderful things that can be accomplished in the quiet, wee hours of the *morning*.

MAGNESIUM

Magnesium really is a miracle mineral, yet it is estimated that approximately 80 percent of Americans are magnesium deficient, according to *The Magnesium Miracle*. The reason is that our soil is tragically depleted of vital minerals like magnesium, so our vegetables and crops are, too. Magnesium is nature's great anti-inflammatory for muscle aches, cramps, and pains. Anyone who suffers from Charlie horse cramps is surely deficient in this mineral. Magnesium is fantastic for better digestion and elimination, calming heart palpitations, and relieving headaches. Soaking in an Epsom salt (magnesium sulfate) bath for 20 minutes allows your skin to absorb the mineral and your muscles will begin to chill out. Foods highest in magnesium are seaweed, coriander, dried pumpkin seeds, raw cacao, almonds, flaxseed, and kale.

In *The Magnesium Miracle*, Carolyn Dean lists many of the ailments that extra magnesium can positively affect:

- Anxiety and panic attacks,
- Asthma,
- Blood clots,
- Bowel disease,
- Depression,
- Detoxification,
- Diabetes,
- Fatigue,
- Heart disease,
- Hypertension,
- Hypoglycemia,
- Insomnia,
- Kidney disease,
- Liver disease,
- Migraines and headaches,
- Musculoskeletal conditions,
- Nerve problems,
- Obstetrical and gynecological issues,
- Osteoporosis,
- Raynaud's syndrome, and
- Tooth decay.

It's always best to check with your doctor before adding new supplements into your diet. There are many forms of magnesium on the market today and some are more specialized for certain conditions. Magnesium sulfate is Epsom salt or milk of magnesia. Magnesium carbonate has antacid properties whereas magnesium citrate includes citric acid and can have strong laxative effects. Magnesium taurate includes the amino acid taurine and can provide a calming effect on your body and mind. I take between 400 to 800 mg of magnesium glycinate in the evening after dinner and in addition to everything else it does, it also helps me to get a better night's sleep. It is highly absorbable and can correct a deficiency. When I get cramps of any kind, I know I have slacked off.

When it comes to bone health, magnesium supplementation is crucial. America is a dairy, cheese, and ice cream-loving nation, yet we have some of the highest rates of osteoporosis. The imbalanced ratio of calcium, magnesium, vitamin D3, and vitamin K2 in our diets has become associated with heart attacks, strokes, and brittle bones. There are many great bone blend supplements available. Two of my favorites are Jarrow Formulas® and Garden of Life®.

Chronic stress depletes your body of vital nutrients, so leave it out on the counter or write in on your bathroom mirror for a reminder of a little self love. All in favor of better rest, no headaches, bowel regularity, and good health, say I! Don't let chronic stress kick your butt—fight back!

MAKEUP

You may be wondering how makeup applies to loving yourself to health. It's pretty simple…less is more! I think increasingly more people—men and women alike—are embracing natural beauty as opposed to a heavily made up face. Not enough people know that the greatest makeup isn't in the department store, it's in the grocery store. Why spend a fortune on massively marketed creams and gels for skin care, when the real care should come from the inside out? Make up ads are far from reality. I think natural beauty is very sexy, really healthy, and a more desirable way to look no matter what your age.

The trick to healthy skin that can go sans makeup is eating and drinking the right foods. Genetics and hormones play a small role—but don't kid yourself—your daily habits play a larger one. The triggers for bad skin are smoking, alcohol, sugar, dairy, and caffeine. In addition to an outward glow, the ultimate side effect of a healthier skincare regime is that your internal organs get a much needed cleanse. If you can't eat it, why would you put it on your skin?

Once I began learning about skin, its function, and how to keep it healthy for a lifetime, all of the positive research I found pointed to using Earth-derived ingredients, not man-made products. Things like aloe vera, olive oil, grape seed oil, vitamin C, and coconut oil seem to be tremendously beneficial for skin tone, wrinkles, softness. They also contain potent antiaging properties.

Changes can take months, but I promise you that it's worth the wait. You will become more radiant in the process and you will learn which trigger foods are causing your breakouts. When you live in a stressful environment that you can't always control, you have to control what you can, and that means what you eat and drink. Take some of those dollars you would spend on so-called beauty products and put them toward organic foods.

I invested in a Clarisonic® skin brush, and it helps to keep my skin clean and soft, especially after a hot yoga class! In the yoga community, no one wears make up to class. It's beauty at its finest—confident, strong, and honest. I use Brallywood Butta® moisturizer from Pristine Beauty® (www.shoppristinebeauty.com) because it's all natural and nourishes my skin. I like my skin now even as I age. I think my mind shift is due to equal parts healthy living and finally embracing my age.

Bella, let your natural beauty shine! Remember, the best products for your skin are basic, edible, and inexpensive.

MEDITATE

I chuckle at the scene from the movie *Eat Pray Love* where Julia Roberts travels to India and experiments with meditation. It is so spot on with how many of us perceive it. If you have ever tried to meditate, initially you may have thought, *Holy crap, I have SO many other things that I can be doing right now!* Yet you were intrigued by the thought of having no thoughts, but it just wasn't working for you! A million random thoughts buzzed through your mind: *How long do I cook the turkey for dinner tonight? Wow, that ceiling fan is really loud. Do I need to stop for gas? I have to pee.* You are not alone. I once stood...well, sat criss-cross applesauce...right where you are.

In today's world, there are increasingly more people who need antianxiety drugs, sleeping pills, and blood pressure medicine. They are enduring stress piled upon stress. Some of it is self-inflicted by making poor choices, but much of it isn't. Deepak Chopra says that for thousands of years people have used meditation to move beyond the mind's busy activity and emotional turbulence into profound peace and expanded awareness. At www.chopra.com you can learn more about the process and how to do it. Like anything else, the more you try it, the easier it will become.

A meditation can be done in as little as 10 minutes and is a fantastic way to start the day. It is not about forcing your mind to be quiet; it's about recognizing that there is always peace and quiet among the noise in your head. You just have to find it. It's not about turning your thoughts off. It's about recognizing that you have a thought, wave goodbye to it, and watch it leave your head, sort of like a banner across the CNN screen. You see the thought, you acknowledge it, and then you let it go. This happens all while you take deep breaths in through your nose and out through your nose. When you do this, your stress hormone levels fall, and so does your blood pressure. You can breathe and find peace anywhere once you know how to do it. In traffic jams, on scary roller coasters, during business meetings, and at home are all places that can bring you more peace if you learn to allow it in.

For me—and at this point in my life—I can meditate pretty easily regardless of what is going on around me. That takes practice, though. Morning is still my favorite time to meditate. Eastern philosophy supports that; between 4:00 a.m. and 6:00 a.m. is when we are most spiritually open to quieting the mind, and allowing for the divine to whisper to us to gently nudge us back onto the track that we must find faith to follow.

Meditation has helped me to function and follow the path that I am called to follow. When you meditate, pay attention to the images, thoughts, and gut feelings that surface. The Lord works in mysterious ways; quiet your mind so you can listen to what He has to say.

MOM

A mom makes a house a home. A mom is the queen bee because she lives with gusto and her love for her children is endless.

My mother Theresa is one such lady. What do I mean by that? She is elegant, classy, beautiful, hardworking, respectable, loyal, faithful, and every single bit of the woman I can only strive to be. She makes me laugh so hard and has loved me whole-heartedly through every year of my life. She is the grandmother whose lap all eight grandchildren would sit on together if they could. My sisters and I watch her be a loving, supportive wife in the ways she honors her marriage to my dad.

When the day came for me to let my mom into my reality of my toxic marriage, I was glad I did. I knew her heart was breaking but she stayed strong for me. She never gave up on me and always brought me back to honoring myself, just like I honor my own children. She kept reminding me that living doesn't mean completely ignoring my own needs. She encouraged me to live the way I want my children to live. My mother listened when it was hard to, stayed on the phone a little longer when I needed her to, and was always there for me with no questions and no judgments.

We need these types of female power houses in our corner. Who in your life can be this for you? It may not be your mother—she could be any strong feminine energy source that has taken on this role in your life. Who has your back when no one else does? Who loves you *unconditionally*? What do you admire about her? Have you told her how you feel? Find your mamma and give her a big kiss on both cheeks—with gusto!

MONEY

> *The problem with money is it often costs too much.*
> —Ralph Waldo Emerson

As far as money is concerned, I write from a very middle of the road perspective—I'm neither homeless nor a billionaire. It sounds basic, but in order to live a happy life with gusto means not spending more than you make, and making the most of what you earn. Many of us don't know how to live within our means. We live like we make five times more than we do and we have debt up to our eyeballs. Debt equals stress, and don't we have enough of *that* already?

Life should have financial priorities—pay the mortgage, buy groceries, pay the bills—but also should include the occasional splurge. I've never been an extravagant individual who needs brand-name everything; my splurge is travel. It's not that I relish sitting in a tiny seat on a stinky plane, but rather who is at the other end of that flight to meet me. Healthy food is the other area where I splurge. Organic produce costs more but is free of many herbicides, pesticides, and fungicides, and tastes a million times better than conventionally grown produce.

My son's great grandmother, Grandma Josephine, tells a story about how her father made $15 a week in 1920s Brooklyn. There was a day when she showed up at his work to ask him a question. She thought she would get in trouble for showing up, but when he came over, but he knelt down and handed her a nickel to spend at the candy shop. When she tells this story, the light in her eyes makes me feel like I am hearing this story from the 10-year-old Italian girl she used to be. The point is they valued what they earned and appreciated every last nickel.

Rest assured that I am not saying spending is bad. I imagine that if I had millions, I would frequently book a first-class seat to Rome just to dine at Mirabelle's while the sultry sun dips behind the horizon of St. Peter's Basilica. The trick here is to not only make sure you can afford it, but to have most of your purchases provide a return of joy for yourself and for others. Excited eyes on Christmas morning because of gifts you gave, airline tickets, concerts with friends, and spending extra on organic ingredients for your special family dinner are all things that are *worth it*.

Moving forward in your life, begin to re-evaluate your relationship with money. Pause for a moment before buying something in the exact same way you should pause before you eat an entire ice cream sundae. Both monetary and food indulgences can be equally as derailing to your future self. Just a penny for my thoughts.

MORNING

During the most stressful parts of my toxic relationship, I barely slept. Night upon night I lay on my pillow, and it was as if every single worry or concern I had during the day was lying right beside me. I envisioned these thoughts as evil monsters, sticky blobs, or even tombstones. Creepy, right? I would think about my kids and their past, present, and future. I would ponder the endless scenarios that could play out in my own present and future.

Despite my nights bringing me precious little sleep, I began to love the mornings. I often felt like a zombie and was entirely exhausted, but I found zero use in lying in bed at 5:00 a.m. with my thoughts spinning. It's one thing to feel tired, but it's another to feel tired *and* have a to-do list the size of Texas. So I decided to get up and grab the day by its grapefruits. I began to embrace my quiet mornings, and you can too! You will be absolutely amazed at how much you can get done in the wee hours of the morning. Replying to work emails, cooking a spaghetti squash in the oven, writing in your journal, enjoying a predawn meditation or a quiet cup of coffee, knocking out a chapter in the book you are reading, banking online, collecting your thoughts, watching the news, or just sitting in the quiet watching the Christmas tree lights twinkle. With this type of start to your day, you become as prepared as possible for the onslaught of toxic relationship sludge you will face during the coming day. Those quiet mornings recharge your draining battery, even with less than subpar sleep.

Mornings can become your time to restore your wherewithal so you can get through the day—days where you want to change the locks, put all of his clothes into the street, or just pack your bags and leave. Use your mornings as a way to love yourself to health. Tomorrow morning when your only prayer is for rest, get out of bed and create your own morning ritual that's filled with centeredness, peace, and checking things off your to-do list. Remember, these are the things that help to manage blood pressure. The rest of the day is going to happen, so why not fortify yourself with a little morning self-love? You need your strength however you can get it, and being kind to yourself means charging your own battery before you can charge everyone else's.

MUSIC

Music can rejuvenate your spirit in so many ways. Some songs give you the power to forget, others the power to remember, to move on, or to stop and refocus. Whether you need to hear a song for its words to remind you that you are strong, or whether you need to just hear music that would make you an emotional hot mess, use music as a tool. It can lift your mood when reality is pulling your world down, and its calorie free! Use it to mentally escape from negativity, and during those times when you need to hear *Hang on tight sweetheart, the best is yet to come!*

I listen to an acoustic version of Alicia Keys "Empire State of Mind" when I need a good cry because I am missing home. I have a *Sinatra* playlist that includes artist like Michael *Bublé*, Diana Krall, Harry Connick, Jr., Ella Fitzgerald, and of course the Rat Packer himself, Frank Sinatra. Then there is my Italian playlist. These plunk me down right down in New York's Little Italy in as a teenager with a curfew of midnight. I even have a *Screw Men* play list that includes a modern version of Gloria Gaynor's "I Will Survive" and Destiny's Child's "Survivor" for when I need to feel empowered. The title of my playlist might be a little snarky, but when I hear Alicia Keys sing "Girl on Fire," I get fired up in all the right ways! I have a soothing playlist with lots of instrumental songs, and other playlists of various genres. I'm partial to acoustic versions because they sound so much earthier.

Go through your tunes and create playlists based on your moods so that when the feeling strikes, you can go inward and get strength or feel free. Spend some time this week reconnecting with your former and evolved self, and find those songs that had you dancing around the room as a teenager singing into your hairbrush or slow dancing with a special someone. Tap into the magic within a melody and allow your heart to sing to you.

Bruschetta…
It's what's for happy hour
with Mom and Dad

The most abundantly
beautiful produce stand
just happens to be in
Duck, North Carolina

A corner of Mother Earth
where I am one with
"Destination Zero"

Seeing this in
Charleston, South Carolina
was lovely, yet "feeling it"
was even more awesome

My parents in Times Square,
New York City – Because
Love should be FUN

The greatest gifts at Christmas time cannot be wrapped

One of our many
matching jammie sets
that we all still have

A gusto filled dinner amid
the hills in Tuscany

Stay centered, stay grounded, stay you

Created with love by Karen Davis Macdonald (kdmartistry.com)

Dinner with Domenic

Me and my girl Lily

Draw your line in the sand

Put your old lipstick to good use

N

On the road to loving yourself to health, you encounter several *N*s. Is your *nest* a comfortable and welcoming place for you and your little birdies? Do you have peaceful sleep at *nighttime*? Have you found your *no*? It might be time to add it to your vocabulary.

NEST

If an hour at the salon can make you feel amazing, just wait until how much more creative and passionate about life you'll feel once you start fluffing up your "nest." Organize it and claim it as your own! Or if it's time to leave it, savor the good memories you built there as you shake off the dust and head out to your new nest.

I have moved several times in my life, but my last one was definitely among the most difficult. Before my divorce, I lived in a beautiful home in a gorgeous neighborhood. We grew lilies, violets, and hydrangeas, and tended an herb garden teaming with three different types of basil, cilantro, oregano, tomatoes, dill, mint, parsley, and rosemary. There was this seemingly magical stone walkway from the deck where our kitty would rest in the afternoon sun. Sometimes I would wish that the walkway would drop me somewhere else at the end of it, far away from the crappy emotional state I was in.

My nest was so cozy, and I loved the big windows in the kitchen where, even on cloudy days, the sunlight came in. I loved to have a fire crackling in the fireplace on cold wintery nights. We even updated the kitchen. I'm not one to get excited over appliances, but I do think that induction stove was pretty sweet.

It made cooking more enjoyable for me, especially on days that weren't.

After I moved, I began to build a new nest that would inspire me to live a more peaceful life and to create new memories. I wouldn't have it any other way because what makes a nest a place of peace is that the little birdies want to be in there. My delicate flower Lily picked out what she wanted in her new room so that she could feel safe, warm, and claim ownership over her new space. She is proud of what she created and enjoys the comfort that her new four walls bring to her. I don't really miss the induction stove either. The "heat" that came with it was not worth my emotional well-being. The memories that have been made here are already far too priceless to trade for a loveless home with better appliances.

Stop and look around your nest. What can you do to reclaim it? Maybe it is just buying fresh flowers? Or possibly a fresh coat of colorful paint will bring more serenity? Maybe it is moving pictures around, and even taking down others. Fluff up *your* nest because it will bring you peace on nights when you feel like you have none. Allow your children to add their personal touches to their own space. Things like that go along way on the comfort scale of life.

NIGHTTIME

I used to feel so restless at nighttime, but not so much anymore. Now I use this time to write or to sleep soundly.

Nighttime is when you should wind down your hectic day and feel relaxed. I strongly recommend you let go of the *married people sleep together* philosophy. Just like the Dementors in *Harry Potter*, nighttime demons will try to suck out any possibility of a sweet dream you may have. You don't have to sleep next to a mean person.

Stay strong and claim your space. Ask the negative person to leave or find your own sacred space where no intruders are allowed. Your health is directly tied to your sleep, as is your weight. Protect it and don't let someone who has little to no respect for you steal your dreams…literally.

NO

It took me a very long time to learn how to say *no*. I found out that it's even better to let your actions speak for themselves. Maybe it was when I said *no* to that phone call that was going to leave me feeling verbally abused or when I said *no* to going to that party where I felt as if I were just the designated driver.

I understand that being in a toxic relationship has led you down a path that you never thought you would be on. You give, you overlook, you ignore, you accept, you are a human filter through which the dirtiest filth can pass and come out the other end looking and smelling like a rose. Because of your love, hope for change, and true desire for peace, your actions have screamed, *Yes! I will accept whatever crap you throw my way because I have become a doormat for you to wipe your feet on!*

No has the power to change your situation. Getting to that place inside you requires a delicate balance of staying ethical and getting ugly (as in strong, bitchy, furious, and armed and ready). Up until now, you have done everything within your power, including compromising your beliefs, in order to have an amicable situation, but you just can't anymore. It's not working.

No, however, can be very expensive. Fighting a battle or really becoming solid and grounded in your beliefs can be costly. Legal fees, moving costs, and other monetary bills associated with "Operation I Call BS" add up. Saying no usually means that you are no longer accepting unsavory behavior and that you are hiring the right people to enforce your position. And that, Bella, is worth every penny.

Take it to another level: do you want your children to see you as a woman who has given up because life has beaten her down? By saying no, you can show your children you've got their backs through the fire of whatever comes your way. Walking through that fire can be terrifying, but by saying no, you *show* your children that your devotion to them cannot be burned, charred, or destroyed. In fact, you can become an example of strength by saying no to such degrading treatment.

Stay clear, focused, and patient as you begin to find your no. Surround yourself with Team Support—your family, friends, lawyers, mediators, and private investigators. Your *no*s will be heard or felt, loud and clear.

O

Redefine your *O!* Go *organic* whenever you can. It's worth the investment in your health. Is it time to *organize* your life, starting with that pile on the kitchen table? You'll get that feeling of a clean mind as well as a clean and organized space.

ORGANIC

Navigating through the hows and whys of organics can be insanely confusing and expensive. It costs money to be well in America, but in the end, it costs far more to be sick. This is truly another area of your wellness that you have a huge amount of control over. Many of my clients cannot initially see the value in buying organic apple A when conventionally grown apple B is bigger, shinier, and cheaper. Then they learn about all of the herbicides, pesticides, and fungicides that apple B has been doused with and what those toxic substances do to their bodies. Those same people cannot understand why it's better to buy grass-fed beef when it costs twice as much as conventionally produced beef.

The manpower and resources that go into keeping animals healthy and raised organically and produce grown organically can be astronomical, and unfortunately, that cost gets passed onto you, the consumer. Organic labeling is big business these days and it is a very expensive and extensive process in order to become USDA certified product. That said, there are many small farmers throughout the country that are chemical free and yet just cannot afford the USDA Organic certification. So, when you shop at your local farmers' market, ask the farmers what they use on their produce. Then do your homework.

Organic grass-fed cattle, although being raised ultimately for consumption, are living the life God intended complete with sunlight, fresh and clean water, grassy pastures providing nourishment, and no antibiotics. Conventionally farmed cattle (and other animals) are raised with zero thought for the animal's well-being and 100 percent thought for the farm's bottom line. They are separated from their young at birth, have minimal drinking water that oftentimes contains sewage runoff, and are fed corn laced with toxic chemicals to get them as fat as possible as fast as possible. Because of close quarters, disease is rampant, so cattle are given a steady dose of intense antibiotics throughout their lives. They are slaughtered so quickly that often their intestines are ruptured during butchering and fecal matter gets into the meat. How's that burger taste now? The same methods hold true for organic veggies and fruits—organic irrigation with clean water or conventional with sewage runoff. Which do you prefer?

Learn ways to free yourself from toxic overload by checking out a few of my favorite sites. You will learn about what chemicals are in your foods and your body care products. Make informed decisions about what you eat by researching, reading, and learning.

- www.ewg.org
- www.michaelpollan.com
- www.foodpolitics.com
- www.organicconsumers.com

Invest in your health by purchasing organic apples, strawberries, grapes, cucumbers, bell peppers, peaches, and celery—they are regulars on the "clean 15" list of what to always buy organic. Eggs, chicken, beef, dairy are all things to consider spending more money on. When you retrain your taste buds to like real food and not junk, you'll crave more of the good stuff. It can be daunting and expensive to go organic all at once, so choose the items that your family consumes regularly and begin with those. Organic doesn't mean less taste, it just means no chemicals! This is a place where anything you do is far better than doing nothing at all. Having said that, not all conventional food products are "bad" which is why as a consumer, you must conduct your own research.

ORGANIZE

When life's emotional clutter consumes you and leaves you feeling out of control, it can be helpful to control what you can. Purging unhealthy relationships from your life is one way to claim control. Organizing your physical space and cleaning out what is no longer serving you is another. I always feel better when I do this and yet I always seem to put off the task. Maybe it's making the time to sit down and go through that pile of mail that puts me off. I could be at yoga class, after all. Or maybe it's clearing the flotsam and jetsam of life from the dining room table that I find daunting. I find, however, whenever I tackle these less-than-fabulous tasks, I always feel a lot better about myself and my situation.

Maybe this is the week to get into your closet and take a few bags to a local charity. Is your email inbox brimming with junk mail that needs to be trashed? Does your kitchen pantry need a sort and a scrub? Organizing your thoughts, your clothes, your emails, and your files all add up to being vital in the greatest detox of your life.

P

During my toxic relationship, I found these *P* items to be incredibly beneficial to maintaining my good health and positive attitude. Find your *passion*. Trust your *private investigator* and trust in the *process* that you will eventually find the peace and happy life you so truly deserve. Tend to your *plants* so your personal living space stays healthy and pretty. Take time for *prayer* and ask your higher power for guidance during your times of struggle. And remember to take your *probiotics* to maintain a healthy gut!

PASSION

Most of us think of passion as being synonymous with physical love and lustful sex. Admit it, even if for a hot second, your thoughts do take you there. Passion really means the trait of being intensely emotional or any object of warm affection or devotion. I am profoundly passionate about writing this book with the hope that you will be able to uncover your own devotion to yourself. (Ok, now, imagine adding a dollop of that lustful passion to the mix. Wow!)

Passions are born out of pure love, like being passionate about wanting to be a good role model for your kids. Sadly, some passions are born from enduring great despair, such as MADD (Mothers against Drunk Driving). Tragedy can unfold into a passionate dedication for a cause that would otherwise not resonate with you on such a deep level.

What are you passionate about? What are you going to do to feed it? Don't starve yourself of what makes you feel alive. Play that piano, pick up the paintbrush, enroll in that class. Say *yes* to that date if you want to. It is now or quite possibly never.

PLANTS

Lovely green plants can not only beautify visually your space, they also can be instrumental in purifying the air quality in your home. The very fact that they bring life into synthetic spaces covered with paint, carpets, and other "dead" areas is enough for me to want to always have a few fabulous leafy friends in my living space.

The chemicals in our surroundings seep into our bodies every single day. Formaldehyde leeches from some carpets, upholstery, and paints. Benzene is found in synthetic fibers, plastics, and rubbers. Trichloroethylene is found in rug stain removers, adhesives, and more. Some plants can even help with carbon monoxide, which is a deadly odorless gas. Plants that can help eliminate toxins that can cause cancer, asthma, and allergies? Bring it!

You have enough toxic crap in your relationship. Do you want more in the air that fills your lungs? Clean out some of the gunk with a few house plants that will detox your air:

- Peace Lily
- Dracaena
- Bamboo Palm
- Golden Pathos
- African Violet
- English Ivy
- Areca Palm
- Rubber Tree Plant

Specialists in the field recommend grouping them together in the corner of different rooms for maximum air purity. Mother Nature doesn't mess around when it comes to clearing the air.

PRAYER

Daily prayer was and is a biggie for me. Prayer is as common in my daily routine as brushing my teeth or choosing something to wear. Prayer can bring to mind many images: a local church mass, an ill person in a bed with a loved one kneeling beside them, or a child saying, *Dear God, please help me pass this test.* Even Tiny Tim saying, *God bless us, everyone.*

My prayers are often prayers of thanks, because it seems to me that no matter what may be tugging at me in the shadows of my life, there is always something to be grateful for. Things like healthy kids, a warm bed, wholesome food, loyal friends, an enjoyable career, sunny days, and soothing music are just a few things that I never stop appreciating. I find traditional Christian prayers, such as The Lord's Prayer or the Our Father, are beautiful and grounding as much as they are reminders of my own humanity and my ability to forgive (but not forget).

The anguish of living in a toxic relationship sometimes can be enough to derail anyone on their journey of faith. Some days it seems impossible to find that silver lining. Together with a community or alone, connect to something larger than yourself and witness a miracle as your thoughts become your words, and your words become your actions. Prayer can shift the direction of your thoughts, slow your heart rate, inspire you to breathe deeper, help you focus on positive things, and even help you fall asleep. Anytime is prayer time.

I find it comforting to know that God answers all prayers. Sometimes the answer is *no*, though, for reasons only the Lord knows. No matter what or if you have a religious affiliation, handing your troubles to a higher power—be it God, Yahweh, Allah, or the Great Spirit—can release you from your mental bonds and free your spirit so you can relish the life you've been blessed with.

PRIVATE INVESTIGATOR

A private investigator is an essential person to have on your support team if there are untruths in your toxic relationship. It's their job to find truth. All of the wondering, all of the second guessing, all of the times you bit your tongue in order to keep things peaceful for the sake of your family unit leads to the moment your private investigator spills the beans. This information can be jarring and ugly. What you do with that information, though, is up to you. You need to make important decisions based on facts, not on heresy or emotion, and your private investigator will help you unearth those facts.

It reminds me a scene from *The Simpsons Movie* where Marge tells Homer something that was quite profound and reflective of how I was feeling at that moment. She said, *Lately, what's keeping us together is my ability to overlook everything you do.* Wisdom from a blue-haired cartoon character? Who knew?

Do you overlook everything? Even things that you know inside and out that are wrong to accept? Your private investigator will help you come to the realization that some people choose to bury their heads in the sand and ignore the truth. But not you. You knew you were on the tip of the iceberg, which is an extremely petrifying place to be. Truth—it's what's for dinner.

Now go on with your bad self, and surround yourself with a team of intelligent people who can help you deal with the dirt. I'm proud of you! Your authentic life awaits your arrival. You just need to trust in the process and believe in the truth. It really will set you free but only after it pisses you off.

PROBIOTICS

Similar to organics, probiotics are another hot topic. Antibiotic means anti-life, whereas probiotic means—you guessed it—pro-life. When we have an infection, we take antibiotics to kill the "bad" bacteria...but they also kill the "good" bacteria, which can leave candida (those bodies of yeast that cause itchy fungal infections) to go wild in your body and depress your immune function. Probiotics help our digestion and immune system function optimally.

Antibiotics, smoking, excessive alcohol, sugar, processed food, and chronic stress are all murderers of our little friendly bugs. It's a game of good cop and bad cop and we want the good guys to win. Having a healthy gut is paramount to a healthy body. These healthy probiotic bacteria go to work in our digestive tract to help balance the healthy flora in our gut. When healthy flora abounds, we digest food better, absorb more nutrients, stay regular, have fewer cravings and clearer skin, and ward off bacteria and viruses quicker. It also means less acid reflux, less bloating, less diarrhea, and less constipation.

Advertising companies spend millions to convince us to buy the new and improved products with unpronounceable strings of probiotics. You can waste your precious dollars if you don't know how to shop for probiotics. With probiotics, you get what you pay for. It helps to remember that probiotics are alive, and things like heat and exposure to air kill them. A good probiotic contains various strains of healthy bacteria. Some to look for on the package are acidophilus, bifidobacteria, and lactobacillus.

Of course you should check with your doctor before taking any supplements. For adults, I usually recommend a dosage containing 8 to 10 billion per day, which usually equates to one to three capsules per day depending on the brand. My local compounding pharmacy has a great one that is 20 billion organisms in one capsule! Probiotics are great to take for 30 days after you finish a dose of antibiotics to rebuild the immune system, and then taper that down to a maintenance phase of about half. Always follow the dosage directions and whether it should be taken with or without food. Some require refrigeration, too. You never want to take out a few and put them in a baggie for travelling because air kills them and that is a complete waste of your money. Some are specifically sealed for traveling, so use those on your next trip and leave the big jar in the refrigerator at home.

There are great children's versions that come in powder that you can add to their drinks, or as chewables or gummies. Find what your children like and make it part of their routine. I really like Garden of Life®, Jarrow Formulas®, and Country Life® products. Usually the ones at the corner store are a waste of money, but research for yourself and put a tiny but fierce army of friendly flora to work for you. Bella, you're only as healthy as your gut!

PROCESS

Your entire toxic situation is such a tricky and confusing road to navigate. Breaking free when your life is intertwined with someone else's is no small endeavor. You may dream of a day when you can feel carefree, safe, and untouched by fear. I understand just how overwhelming and frightening this unchartered abyss is.

The super-highway of your brain is congested with a never-ending traffic jam of how, who, where, and when. Thoughts of kids, money, friends, explanations, perceptions, realities, lawyers, proof, future, and so much more pile up on that highway. You must believe that this too is a process, and the direction in which you are heading eventually will become clear.

Try not to fantasize about how things are going to unfold because it rarely materializes the way you envision it will. Instead, continue to surround yourself with the necessary support from friends and industry experts. Stay focused on your work and those you love. The process will be revealed. Sometimes you may take a wrong turn, but just keep listening to your gut because the answers first come disguised as inexplicable feelings that make no sense yet. But they will, I assure you.

Now's a good time to take a breather in a nice, warm Epsom salt bath, pour a glass of wine or tea, light a candle, and trust in the process. Add to that a sprinkle of patience and a prayer, and you will be further along today than you were yesterday. One day, clarity and truth will lead the way through the process and many of your questions will be answered. But for now, be still, and trust that the Divine Spirit is working in tandem with yours.

Q

Q is quick! Actually, *Q* is for *quit* and *quote*. Both have the power to set you free when you're feeling vulnerable or empty.

QUIT

You didn't grow up fantasizing about the day you end your relationship. Yet here you are at the crossroads facing that very decision. You've come to that time after you've stayed, smiled, exuded grace, and forgave. You laughed in public, cried in private, and put on a happy face so that those you love would never be burdened. You showed up for work meetings fully present, and you rolled up your sleeves and gave until you realized that giving more means living less. Then and only then did you realize that sometimes it's perfectly okay to quit.

I'm here to tell you that it's okay to quit. Quitting a bad relationship doesn't mean you are quitting on your children, your family, or yourself. It means you are making a decision for yourself and your children that your health and happiness are more important than saving face and keeping up false appearances of a "happy" life.

Although it is true that some may throw in the towel much too early on a relationship that could have been saved by a communication and reality infusion, this is not you. The only towel you are throwing in is the one that is getting tighter and tighter around your neck. You are choosing the path of a more harmonious life instead of continuing on a path of guaranteed sadness, misery, and ill health. You are resilience personified. You can do this, Bella, because loving yourself to health means choosing life over a slow death.

QUOTES

Oh, how I love a good quote. I especially like the ones that really drive a point home, and the ones that make me feel empowered over my situation. Find ones that inspire you and write them where you will see them regularly, like on your bathroom mirror in lipstick! These little affirmations can strengthen your inner child when you need that little boost.

There are hundreds of quotes that I look to when I need that boost—quotes by Rumi, *Elie Wiesel*, Victor Hugo, and Oscar Wilde to name a few. But ultimately, my favorite quote has to be LOVE IS PATIENT, LOVE IS KIND.

R

I really don't believe diamonds are a girl's best friend—it's a good book to *read*. *Relatives* can be a big source of support and strength for you—but they also come with perspectives and biases that may not be in your best interest. Your journey is much like that of the *river rock*—you may feel thrown around and tumbled now, but you'll emerge from the riverbank shiny and new. Sometimes a good *road trip* is what you need to unwind—company recommended but optional. The most important *R* is *research*—arming yourself with knowledge will protect your interests and fortify your spirit.

READ

Before I became a Certified Health Coach, I already had an expansive knowledge base surrounding all sorts of foods and healing modalities. When my free time allowed me to put my nose into a book, I loved to read one type of genre: health. I would read about food, vitamins, research, and all things that made me a more informed advocate for my clients. What I hadn't realized was that I needed a break from health topics. My "all day" topics were becoming my "all night" topics.

One day my beautiful and loving friend left *The Help* by Kathryn Stockett in my mailbox. I had forgotten just how refreshing it was to read a novel and not a nutrition label. I became absorbed in the characters' fears, marriages, lives with their children, their passions and causes, and their laughter and sorrows. For just an hour, I forgot about the cross I carried daily that was breaking my own heart.

So find something to read that's off your own beaten path, and allow of yourself to escape your everyday grind, rise above it, and fly away, even if just for a little while.

RELATIVES

When there is stress in your relationship, you may find that relatives can be a source of tremendous emotional strength. Or you may find that relatives offer you inappropriate advice based on their own perspective of what they think your relationship is. What I mean by this is they only see the image that your toxic spouse puts out there. You know that image is a big untruth...but they don't. They may not understand just what is going on in your marriage and why you'd ever want out. Odd as it may seem, your stress can be very emotional for them because they may feel they have to choose sides or that they need to protect someone's image.

When listening to their advice, it's imperative that you consider the source. Do you want marriage advice from the man who's cheating on his wife? Do you want marriage advice from the woman bearing a grudge against her ex of 10 years? Ask yourself who you want to take advice from—the happy people or the miserable people?

I suggest you only reach out the people who really love you and support your well-being, not just the image of what they think your marriage should be. Stay away from those who have lopsided thinking and ignore the facts. Don't waste your time listening to half-baked advice from irrational people. Identify who is with you and who is not. Ally yourself with relatives who are living in truth, and see the facts for what they are. Disassociate yourself from those in complete denial and those who can't handle the truth. These can be scary times, but they don't have to be for you if you surround yourself with relatives and loved ones who will support you and love you regardless of your marital status. Life is tough but you are tougher!

RIVER ROCK

The story of the river rock is quite similar to the story of the lotus flower. The river rock achieves its beauty by being shoved around by every rushing flow of water. The relentless attack from the current, other rocks, waterfalls, and mother nature renders the little rock a sleek and unique beauty that only from hardships and having its butt kicked can it become as perfect as it is. Just like you.

In the flowing currents of the river of your own life, you are that little rock being tossed around for a purpose unbeknownst to you right now. If you acknowledge this and go with the flow of the current, you will become exactly as you are supposed to be. You will become radiant, defined, and unlike any other. You are perfect already, but the process of becoming a river rock will *remind* you that you are.

So take that deep breath, place your right hand over your heart, and tell yourself that you are worth every single bump and twist. Add to that a firm stance on staking out what is true and moral for you, surround yourself with people who want you to evolve, and you will come out of the depths of the river more whole than when you went it. You are smooth, you have weathered the transformation, and you can do this.

ROAD TRIP

Maybe what you need is a road trip. It doesn't even have to be overnight, just long enough to laugh a little and listen to some good tunes with good company—even if that company is just you! Just like a latitude adjustment, a road trip is food for the soul. It's more about the journey than the place itself.

I recently left my cares behind on a trip to Charleston to see my son. It was my daughter's birthday weekend, and my parents were along for the adventure. We munched on fresh-baked bread and joined in as Michael Bublé sang "Let It Snow" on that

85 degree October day. We switched to Italian music, which brought us visions of Tuscan vineyards and vibrant streets of Rome. While my dad and my daughter carried on in the back seat, giggling and sharing stories, my mom and I did the same in the front. Other memorable road trips include excursions to soccer games, cab rides through Brooklyn, and rides to the beach or mountains with friends.

Some days you have to dig pretty deep for a bout of joy. Some days though, it's terribly simple. It really is. All it really takes is surrounding yourself with love so that when the dips come, you have the strength to get through it. If you can, treat yourself to a road trip, but be selective about with whom you go. No Debbie downers allowed here. Or just go alone. These are the very moments that recharge your battery and provide you stamina for the drama that will be waiting for you when you get home. It is 100 percent necessary to check out sometimes, or you will become diseased with heavy downtrodden negativity. Look at your calendar, and text a buddy right now. No way is it selfish because life is for the living, and I know how badly you want to *live*.

RESEARCH

Before I shifted gears from *how to stay* to *how to leave*, I felt I was in a dizzying cloud drifting to wherever. Instead of feeling weak and emotionally vulnerable, I gave myself more unconditional love by empowering myself with knowledge. It's amazing how much I learned when I started owning my situations and stopped feeling the victim.

Once the dust settles, and you realize that you aren't in Kansas anymore you stand up, dust yourself off, and begin to research. This can mean searching online for different professionals that can help you, like counselors or lawyers. It can mean sitting in the library or local bookstore reading inspirational books. It can mean networking with trusted social circles (beware of wolves in sheep's clothing here…many folks look like friends but are just nosy, and when you are emotional you can let the wrong people in). Or it can mean visiting a few apartment complexes to get a feel for where you may wind up living.

The research part of your healing process can seem daunting, but the more you learn, the more confident you will feel. Even if you are the brightest, strongest woman, you can sometimes do things that baffle the rational mind when you are stressed and feeling powerless and pushed into a corner. These are but coping mechanisms that you have had to create just to get by. As you discover the answers to the hows and whens, you will fortify yourself with a newfound sense of determination and resilience. Read, review, look up, and find your answers. Knowledge is power, and you, Bella, are one powerful woman.

S

There are many health items associated with *S*—some you need more of and some you don't need at all! *Simplify* your life by reconsidering how much stuff—emotional, physical, and everything in between—you have. Eat more *salads*! *Smile* more and brighten your mood. Eschew *synthetics* but embrace *sweat*. Appreciate your *sisters*, blood or otherwise. *Sing* out loud and proud! Watch your *son* grow from boy to man. *Sleep* more. Eat less *sugar*.

SALAD

Greens are the single most missing food in the American diet today. Think about it. When we dine out at most mainstream restaurants, our meal is typically accompanied by a weak-looking side salad of iceberg lettuce and an unripe garden tomato. How unappealing! Not that I am above boring fruits and veggies, I just know how nutritionally deficient they are. The lack of fiber, protein, and fat leaves me starving!

One day I was making a salad when my son breezed through the kitchen. Before long he realized that it was a salad just for me. He made me crack up with his impromptu jokes about how I was eating an entire garden at once. There you have salad rule number one—double or triple your salad portion size. Just say no to teeny side salads! Here are some guidelines to consider next time you want your salad to keep you full and nourished:

- Double or triple the size.
- Use a variety of green lettuces.

- Chop veggies and lettuce into small pieces. It's much better for your digestion because raw veggies are harder to digest.

- Add proteins like nuts, seeds, chicken, boiled egg, salmon, tofu, tempeh, beans—whatever you like.

- Add fiber like garbanzo beans, steamed broccoli, cauliflower, edamame, beets, and/or avocado.

- Ask for dressing on the side or use fresh squeezed lemon, olive oil, and a little mustard or salt. Use sparingly and toss well before adding more.

- When dining out, look at the entire menu and see if there's something you would like to add to your salad that isn't listed in the salad section. Most restaurants will oblige.

- Think texture! What are you craving?

Lack of dietary greens is one of the reasons we are so magnesium deficient, so take a little extra time to create a colorful dish that will honor your body and all you are trying to accomplish with it. There are many fantastic BPA-free salad containers with separate compartments for dressing and even built in plastic forks and spoons, so traveling with a salad to work or on a plane has gotten so much easier. It's always a better option than a candy bar disguised as a "nutrition" bar. I promise that if you add fiber and protein to you next salad, you will feel more satisfied and less likely to roam around the kitchen for a little something extra.

SIMPLIFY

I think my yoga practice is somehow intertwined with my growing desire to simplify. When practicing yoga, I embrace that it is a "me, myself and I" thing. The only competition is within myself as I struggle to accept my light and dark side, or my fears and inhibitions. It helped me realize that I wanted to get back to myself—unfiltered, raw, and organic Jeanine. The best part is that I have only scratched the surface and I like what I see and feel. The entire process of walking away from a toxic relationship and embracing my career of helping people detox from mean people made me crave a simpler, less complicated life—less complicated dinners, less laundry, fewer bills, less living space to clean, and no more life maintenance that wasn't absolutely necessary.

Living simply means that your true, authentic self can emerge. When that happens, God brings the coolest people back into, or newly, into your life. Sure, there will be residual stuff that you'll have to manage because of the past, but there will be so much more that is new, true, reliable, honest, firm, and good in your life, that it will far outweigh any negative remainders. I love my simplified life, and you will too. The way I see it is that God takes all things off of your plate that don't really matter to your spirit's growth so that you can focus on what does. I really believe God had this silver lining thing down!

SING

For me, singing is a release and can always make me feel so happy—for others within earshot, maybe not so much! I have always enjoyed it, even as a kid, but never took myself too seriously. The darker my life got during my toxic marriage, the more I would sing. It was a given that there was nothing I could do about other people's sour moods. But I could always go back to my free therapy and experience a complete mood shift afterward.

Whether you are in the shower, have Dr. Dre Beats™ headphones on, or are in the car with your children, make a joyful noise. I sing with my daughter all the time in the car. We just laugh about how much we sing and about the wacky lyrics we invent. It doesn't matter what you're singing. Just belt it out, Bella!

SISTERS

I have two older sisters who are twins and I have one younger sister—I'm right in the middle. We are forever bonded because we are the four little princesses who grew up in a kingdom where true love reigned. As adults, our lives took very different turns from each other, but the fabric from which we are woven is the same. Our core values stand firm and alike, and even though we dabbled down life's crazy paths at times, we seemed to all wind up back on the same road, the road seeking peace and simplicity. At this place, we accept one another, hug each other, and never question why or how.

Theresa, I admire you for your simplicity and ability to avoid anything that is not feeding your soul. You are living proof that all that really matters can be found within those we love. Your marriage is beautiful, and I adore your husband Jamie. Dena, I admire you for your tenacity to crave something better in life, and your spunk can carry you through even the darkest days. You are proof that a woman doesn't need a man to be happy, but that the right man can make your spirits soar. Laraine, my baby sister, your ambition and ability to juggle career, marriage, and motherhood is praiseworthy. You are most adept at juggling three crystals balls without dropping one. You are married to your best friend, Chris. I love you all so very much. I am always here for you in heart, body, and soul. May all of our traditions and traits live on in the lives of our children, our greatest and only real legacy worth leaving.

Here you have four different women from the same gene pool. We acknowledge our differences yet can rely on each other *no matter what*. Who is in your sisterhood? You don't need to be related to share a deep and abiding sisterhood with strong women who've got your back.

SLEEP

Getting quality sleep is one of the biggest struggles people have today. It's difficult enough to get to sleep with the normal everyday demands and stresses of life, but when you add a toxic relationship to the mix then the quality of your sleep really goes down the drain. The reality is this: sleep is just as important as what you eat and your level of physical activity. When you sleep, your body processes the nutrients you fed it during the day and puts them to work. Your liver goes to work filtering out the gunk in your body, and its activity peaks around 3:00 a.m. Deep sleep helps your body to restore, repair, and heal from the day's stress and nutritional slaughter.

Have you ever considered the connection between all of the sleeping pills that are prescribed and the amount of coffee that is consumed, or maybe the connection between lack of sleep and the copious amounts of erectile dysfunction drugs prescribed? Remember that hormonal conditions like PMS, menopause, cortisol imbalances, or low testosterone can all affect sleep. So can crawling into bed on a full stomach—you will either sleep or digest what you just ate, but not both! So you're stressed and you're not sleeping well (and maybe you're not getting any lovin'!). How do you begin to get better sleep? If you are consistent in doing the things on the following list, your sleep should improve over the next few nights.

- **Avoid bright lights, TVs, and computers before bedtime.** For the same reasons we don't put babies to sleep around bright lights, we shouldn't do it ourselves. Light reduces the production of the sleep hormone melatonin. Prolonged exposure to artificial lighting only compounds sleep issues. Our ancestors went to bed when the sun when down and got up with the dawn. They read by candlelight and were un-stimulated by technology, which probably explains why there was a whole lot more lovin' going on back then, too.

- **Eat a light snack that contains carbohydrates.** If you need a night time snack, have a few gluten-free crackers with a little almond butter. Carbs help release serotonin, which relaxes us.

- **Take a warm bath.** Add Epsom salt, which is a type of magnesium to soothe sore muscles and help you relax. What's not to love about being alone for 30 minutes to close your eyes and just chill?

- **Cut off all caffeine after 1:00 p.m.** That means don't drink any tea, coffee, chocolate milk, or soda. Extra caffeine keeps you up when you should be calming down.

- **Limit sugar during the day.** For someone who is sugar sensitive, even one chocolate chip cookie after dinner has the power to rev them up. Anyone who's ever seen a kid on a sugar high can attest to this. Why do we think that as adults we are any different?

- **Reduce sleeping pill consumption.** First, always get your doctor's advice on this topic. If you are on prescription sleeping pills, cut them in half or into thirds to begin breaking your dependence on them. They are extremely addictive. Try taking half to fall asleep. Or if falling asleep isn't the issue, but waking at 2:00 a.m. is, try taking half or a third then. Always make sure you have ample time before having to wake and drive. This is a hard addiction to break because you may feel like being knocked out is the only time you aren't sad. Operation Love Yourself to Health requires you to learn how to sleep all on your own.

- **Alter the time of day you exercise.** Sometimes exercising late in the day/evening can wind you up because of additional circulation and oxygenation. Pay attention to how you feel when you exercise in the morning versus the evening. Is there a difference in your ability to sleep?

- **Add magnesium to your diet.** 400 mg of magnesium glycinate in the evening can really help you get to sleep and stay asleep. It's the number one mineral for reducing stress and helps you chill out.

SMILE

The very act of smiling releases good chemicals like serotonin and dopamine within our brains. They say laughter is the best medicine, and from a physiological and emotional stand point, I couldn't agree more! Some days it can seem impossible to smile, and even though there are always blessings to count, there will be days that are filled with so much anguish and abuse that a smile isn't always in the cards. When you have days like that, it can be very helpful to remove yourself from the situation or location.

There were so many times when I left the house to find my smile with a *paesana*. It was inevitable that we would wind up completely hysterical over something that brought humor into both our days. Friends truly possess a magic wand that can turn a big frowny face into a sparkle of renewed hope. They will help you find laughter when you feel like you'll never smile again. A candle never goes out by sharing its light, and true friends won't keep score because they delight in your joy. A smile goes a long way in brightening someone's day. Who can you be with this week that makes you smile? If you can't see them, then call or text them. Smiles travel really well—no refrigeration required. *Ti amo il mio amico.*

SON

My son has been a huge part of this journey for me. I am continually humbled when I stop to realize that my children have the innate ability to teach me about life as much, and sometimes more so, than I teach them. I love that cool parenting moment when I get a glimpse into hearts and minds of my children and really see them for who they've become—when I really see the dreams and hopes that *they* have for themselves. I also find it fascinating to witness nature versus nurture at work when I see how their lifestyle and choices they make come clearly into play.

The day my son was born I held him in my arms, staring into his beautiful dark eyes. Beyond his handsome dark hair and olive complexion, he is a person who is resolute in his beliefs and speaks with conviction on the ideas he feels strongly about. He sings when he's happy and is always cracking a funny joke, but can also be serious and present when he needs to be. He has a fierce loyalty for family and traditions, yet walks to the beat of his own drum. He would rather be in no company than be in bad company. He's lively, positive, has a great work ethic, and adores his little sister even when she's being a pesky little sister.

Domenic, I think you are a type of *brilliant* that cannot be measured on a test. You are endlessly deep, and you have immeasurable gifts to offer this world and the people in it. Keep spreading your light and thank you for eternally lighting mine. You have roots and wings, and that is all I could ever wish for you.

SUGAR

As a Health Coach, I believe sugar is the root of all nutritional evil. Transfats and other chemically altered food-like substances are wicked, but sugar can be worse. Sugar is terribly addictive and the cycle it kicks off only serves to make you continually hungry and eventually makes you fat. The white flour products you consume turn to sugar in your body as quickly as eating a tablespoon of sugar. Why? Because your body is seeking macronutrients—fat, protein, and slow-burning carbs—and those things are missing from the typical chips, rice, white bread, and cookies. So you eat breads and sweet stuff and your body quickly turns that stuff into fast energy…sugar! You continue to eat more because your body isn't satisfied because it isn't getting those macronutrients. So what do you do? Eat *more* bread and sugar. Hence, the vicious cycle continues. Then the pounds begin to pack onto your butt, thighs, and midsection.

Food manufacturers hide sugar in practically everything: juice, wine, cookies, dressings, bread, crackers, chips, soup, spaghetti sauce, condiments, and so many more foods. Flip over the package and read the sugar content. Four grams of sugar equals one teaspoon. Ideally, it is best to limit sugar from fruits and veggies to 25 grams or less per day. For example, one cup of blueberries has about seven grams of sugar. Yes, it is true that sugars from fruits and veggies count as sugar, and it is a myth that fruit sugar, honey, agave, molasses, sugar in the raw are better for you. In all fairness, they do have vitamins and minerals, but the sugar can have the same effect on your insulin levels.

I recently had a client tell me that if sugar were created today, it would probably be in the same category as alcohol and tobacco. I couldn't agree more. The addiction to sugar is super strong and the withdrawal is very real. Coming off sugar leads to moodiness, anger, insomnia, exhaustion, headaches, cold sweats, and fierce cravings. Your spoiled taste buds are like a bratty kid throwing a tantrum—they want sugar and when they don't get it they kick and scream until you give in. The good news is that the detox period is typically short. For some it's as short as three days; for others it can be longer. Once you've detoxed, you'll wonder why you didn't do it sooner. You will adopt a "whatever" sort of attitude about sugar and won't be controlled by it. The rub is that it doesn't take much to become addicted all over again. Two or three days of eating sweets can wake up those screaming taste buds again. The only difference is this time, you'll have caught it before there was 10 extra pounds of damage, messed up hormones, hot flashes, and picked fights with a loved one.

This is one tough habit to kick. It is just as much about biology as it is willpower. With all that is going on in your life, if you are choosing *you* then you must take control of your sugar addiction. Excess sugar in your diet can lead to inflammation in the gut, heart disease, poor liver function, high cholesterol, insomnia, excessive weight gain, and hormone fluctuation. It also can become a nightmare for menopause and diabetes. I work with people all the time who win the battle of the white stuff. You can be one of those people, too. How bad do you want it? Haven't you had enough of feeling sick? You can take control of what you eat.

SWEAT

As I mentioned in *Deodorant* earlier in this book, sweating is great for clearing out the pores and helping detox the body of impurities. Sweating can help relieve water retention from PMS, and the exercise that produces the sweat can improve even the most sour mood by releasing a fresh supply of happy hormones into the brain.

When you sweat, you're obviously going to get dehydrated if you don't replenish your fluids. I recommend that you aim for a minimum daily of half your body weight in ounces. For instance, if you weigh 140 pounds, try to drink at least 70 ounces or more a day. In addition to ridding your body of impurities, sweating also excretes essential minerals like magnesium and salts, so I also recommend you replenish the hydration lost with a good electrolyte-based drink. In the *Hydration* section, I told you about a product named Ultima Replenisher®. It's awesome. One scoop in my water bottle gives me a nice balance of necessary electrolytes to rehydrate my body (www.ultimareplenisher.com).

I get my sweat on with hot yoga. It's a synchronicity of movements in a 105-degree, humid room. If you've ever tried it, you'll know it's impossible to not sweat. Holding deep poses for longer and practicing better alignment both contribute to the intensity of the practice and the more you sweat. Whatever your joy—be it running, basketball, yoga, biking, or cardio at the gym—work up a good sweat as often as you can. Get your heart rate up, zone out from the toxicity in your life, and sweat your way to a clearer mind and a tighter behind!

SYNTHETIC

Siri on my iPhone defines synthetic as *not of natural origin; prepared or made artificially.* Every step I took toward a healthier lifestyle, whether it was eating more greens or less sugar, exercising more, or detoxing from crazy people, resulted in me craving a less synthetic existence. I began using grape seed oil as a moisturizer and coconut oil for hair conditioning treatment, and drinking raw organic aloe vera juice. Months later, as I walked through the department store, I noticed something profoundly different about myself. As I began living a healthier lifestyle, I really began to notice all of the heavily made up faces and the people behind them spending a small fortune on perceived, store-bought beauty. They were missing the point. Real beauty comes from within, not from a blend of a thousand artificial smells or the $38 dollar lipstick. I am not saying that wearing makeup makes you an inauthentic person. Who doesn't like to get dolled up for a special occasion or wear a sexy shoe just for fun?

A less synthetic life to me means living a healthy life, including eating whole unprocessed foods and maybe even growing some of your own herbs and veggies. It means walking barefoot when you can, wearing organic cotton as much as possible, eating foods free from dyes and preservatives, using natural products in your home, and not hanging around with negative people.

In between life's special occasions, I urge you to take off your makeup, remove your shoes off, connect to the Earth (the ground, not the floor), and get a little closer to nature. This will heighten your awareness and fine tune your radar to eschew all things synthetic in your path, including toxic people with hidden agendas. Uncover your beauty and don't darken your light with synthetic living.

T

T holds so much promise. "After all, *tomorrow* is another day," said the newly hopeful Scarlett O'Hara. She was right. Once you reach that point of self-actualization, perhaps a *tattoo* would be just the thing to celebrate your new outlook on life. Life is full of *traditions* that root you to your happy place and give you memories to give to the future generation...what are some of yours? *Transition* is a tough thing to get through, but you're a strong, empowered, and confident survivor. You can make it through this. And after you make your difficult decisions, sit down with a steamy hot cup of *tea* to unwind and relax.

TATTOO

Gone are many of the stigmas associated with tattoos. Many people these days have them. At hot yoga class, you see a lot of skin, and with it, tattoos. For many of us, the ink carries a very deep and personal message. Some tattoos are of simple words, some portray a loved one, and others are images or symbols. Tattoos are as unique as the individuals themselves. Just like Obamacare, abortion, and border control, opinions vary on tattoos, too, and that's okay.

I think those folks in the anti-tattoo camp are just on a very different road than I am. Truth be told, I once walked there. Naysayers may ask how you'll like your tattoo when you're 90 years old. What's funny is that once you don't put your self-worth in your appearance, you don't really give a rat's ass about how it will look when you are 90. Another argument proclaimed by the anti-tattoo group is that they're unprofessional in the workplace. On the contrary, some of my clients are extremely high-level executives and they defy the typical corporate image.

Their individuality seems to be one of their strengths. They are brilliant, focused, driven and—OMG—some even have tattoos! Maybe it's the nonconformity of a tattoo or even that different haircut or color that society has conditioned us to believe is inappropriate in the workplace.

It seems to me that as we age, become healthier, and gain more clarity about our own being, that the body as a canvas for self-expression can be a beautiful thing. For me, once I realized that I was so much more than my outward appearance, getting a tattoo was almost like shedding my skin, in a way. On my right wrist, it says *Love is…* and on my left, it says *Kind.* I will feel that way until the day I die, wrinkles, dentures, saggy tattoos, and all.

TEA

For me, tea is different from coffee, yet some of the comforts from it are similar to coffee: the warmth, the enjoyment of unhurried and relaxed environments, the signal that it's time for "me" time, and that caffeinated boost when the day is pushing me into the ground. Tea tends to be healthier because most people don't add sugar, artificial sweetener, or sweetened or flavored creamers, so right off the bat, it's an improved choice. If I require sweetener in my tea, I will add stevia for a tasty and satisfying treat. Even my daughter enjoys decaf varieties in the evenings sometimes…and that's actually one of our traditions together.

Green teas are very high in antioxidants, yet can taste bitter. If you aren't feeling the love from green tea, try another brand because they are all so different. At that point, if you still don't like it, then don't drink it. A word of warning: too much green tea can have a laxative effect…which some people seem to do cartwheels over. No kidding! Don't forget that many teas can also pack a powerful caffeine punch, so consider the time of day before you sip. Many people who enjoy cold tea like to brew it first and then place the pitcher in the refrigerator. I like the Yogi® ginger tea. It's decaffeinated and tastes delicious cold on a sweltering day.

When your head feels like it's going to explode with apprehension, take a moment to chill out before you say or do something that may damage your exit plans. Recharge your battery with 15 minutes of letting loose—no reading, no talking, and no researching, just sipping tea. Take a lesson from the teabag, and let things steep for a while. Time has a way of changing everything.

TOMORROW

Tomorrow is one of my favorite words in our entire language. Just thinking of tomorrow springs eternal hope in my mind. You have the *opportunity* to do something differently tomorrow than you did today. How encouraging is that? You can say no when you feel like you have to say yes but don't want to, or you can sleep for an extra hour in the morning because today was relentless. You can apologize and make something right, or you can let an idea quietly marinate within your brain.

I am graced with the view of exceptionally exquisite sunrises from the balcony of my apartment, and for living in small town America, it is really quite a gift to see. My view overlooks a cute little pond and weeping willow tree. When the sun rises in the morning, especially in the summer, my entire living room is bright red from its glow. Anyone who's seen a Carolina sunrise over the ocean knows what I mean.

It's ok, Bella, to pack it in and just go to bed early sometimes. Bid farewell to a day that, for whatever reason, didn't turn out as planned, or that just kicked your butt a little too much. Wake up tomorrow and do something different, say something different, contact someone different, confide in someone different, or just think differently. What a gift the sunrise brings with it. That alone holds all the affirmation you need to flourish.

TRADITIONS

With all of the drama going on in your life, now's the time to fiercely protect those traditions that keep you feeling alive and connected to your past. Those deep-rooted moments will constantly provide food and nourishment for your soul as you are feeling chewed up and spit out. In the end, those traditions are all you have to pass on to your children. Years from now, when you are long gone, how will *you* show up in *their* future? Will you be in the music they choose to listen to during the holidays? Will you show up in the desserts they bake with their children? Maybe by thinking of you and your words, they will find super-human strength to carry their own cross in life. Traditions can be so simple, yet allow the weight of a million memories to flood into your heart.

Here are some of my most treasured traditions that I hope my children remember us sharing together, and can someday remain inspired to share with their own loved ones.

- Baking a Happy Birthday Jesus cake for our Christmas Eve celebration.

- Getting frozen yogurt on a hot summer's evening.

- Watching *The Polar Express* at Christmas.

- Watching *CBS This Morning* on a Sunday morning.

- Going for a "snow walk" at night while the flurries gently fall upon us.

- Making up a three-part bedtime story to be told over three nights.

- Adding the perfect amount of chocolate chips in the gluten-free pancakes.

- Saying our prayers together each night.

- Hitting the hiking trail we love throughout all of the seasons.

- Making *arancini* (Italian rice balls) at Thanksgiving.
- Baking *struffoli* (Italian honey balls) at Christmas.
- Waking my children gently in the morning.
- Dancing to and singing along with our favorite songs.

When you wake up in the morning and your significant other has fabricated a reason to be annoyed with you, stay present. Continue with your day as if you don't have a care in the world. Get the children, backpacks, homework, and lunches into the car, and sing with them like you like to do. Choose to make those moments peaceful not only for them, but for yourself. Reply to that work email in a focused, Dementor-free mind. Tradition robbers are right up there with health hackers, and if you surrender the traditions that are important to you then they will spend their lives wanting and demanding more. Raise the rent and evict them from your head! Keep your treasured traditions alive.

TRANSITION

Years ago I read a poem about a flying trapeze. There's this scary space between letting go of one bar in order to grasp the next one. Is there a net below? Is there a seemingly endless ocean below teeming with great white sharks? In those moments of letting go and reaching for something stronger and more reliable, we are faced with the fear of uncertainty, doubt, and an overwhelming feeling of *am I doing the right thing*? Not only are we feeling fear in this space, there is the question of how long will it last. The truth is that taking that leap of transition in the hope of creating something safer for yourself can last for a minute or for 10 years or more. The trapeze bars are laid out before you, swinging in different directions. There may be so many swinging trapeze bars over your ocean of sharks that you feel intimidated and alone and you wonder if you will catch the next bar.

Here is where your faith comes into play. Take that first leap. This leap is realizing that you cannot stay where you are, and is the hardest one because it requires force and energy to create momentum. The realization that you must do this in order to change your life is usually the result of years of pain and anguish before you finally have had enough of the crap that you've been dealt. In all fairness, you stayed in the game, got dealt the hand of junk, but now you are folding out of a poker game where the last laugh has always been on you.

When I told my good friend that I was taking that first leap toward my new, happy life, she began to sing the Kenny Rogers song "The Gambler"—you know, the part about knowing when to walk away or when to run!

Regardless of whether your situation involves kids, emotions, or abuse, you may feel this incredible sense of urgency to just make it all go away…now. You dream of living past the day you tell your children the family is splitting up. You envision the day when you pack your bags and move out. You fantasize about the day that you can know your children feel peace and joy. There is no time limit on this. Sooner rather than later would be lovely, but it doesn't always happen that way. This all brings you back to trusting in the process. Never stop trying to grab onto that first trapeze bar, even if it seems that it's rigged or broken.

Moving out was a huge accomplishment for me, yet it brought on an entirely different set of worries. I worried about my children constantly. The whole process is really very similar to raising a child. When you have a newborn, you worry about SIDS; when you have a toddler, you worry about crossing the street and swimming pools; when you have a teenager, you worry about driving. I have found that if I am waiting for that time when I don't worry, I never will find it. Why? Because it doesn't exist. The worrying really never ends. But tomorrow is a new day. I will reach for the next bar, and leave this one behind. I will pay homage to my fingers and hands for allowing me to press onward and upward.

My dear Bella, take one day at a time, one bar at a time. You are evolving like the lotus flower and the river rock as you transition and persevere through the filth. As you do, you will notice a tiny, shimmery, and sparkly spot that you hadn't noticed before. Keep your eyes, heart, and mind wide open to what your transition will bring to you. It will be the most dazzling thing you have ever felt and will provide you with the momentum needed to reach for tomorrow and beyond.

TRUE NORTH

Where does your inner compass point? Do you feel like it leads you astray or perhaps maybe it's broken? There are millions of people wandering through life with a sort of prosthetic moral compass that, as you guessed it, leads to a very unhealthy decision making process. I have come to know several people who make choices based on how cool, powerful, or attractive *they think they will be* rather than making a choice that is more of a win-win for all involved. In the workplace, this may translate into the coworker who tweaks everything with her own special spin so that she's the one who comes out looking like a hero with no regard for the rest of the team. At home, this could be the spouse who has his lover and wife in the same room at a party. His like-minded "friends" love the rush and drama the whole scenario provides. In both situations, an inability to find your True North results in one self-sabotaging decision after another.

How do you find your True North? Well, it takes a commitment to self-discovery and asking yourself some pretty deep questions. Who are you? What are your life goals? Do you value people more than money? If yes, how do your actions prove this, day in and day out? Anne Bruce—speaker, author, and trainer in human development and personal growth—has taught thousands worldwide to be the author of their own "life story" with her no-nonsense approach in her book *Discover True*

North. Visit www.AnneBruce.com to pick up a copy for yourself, and fine tune your inner compass, Bella. This is how you walk the path you are meant to without winding up in a dead end on the road of life.

U

U is so unique there's only one thing here to do: *unplug*. By that I mean step away from things or people that zap your energy—mentally or physically. It's okay to disconnect from the constant deluge of chatter coming your way 24/7.

UNPLUG

I want to be clear on what I mean by the term *unplug*. Because life is so full of demands—positive and negative—sometimes our coping mechanisms have to kick in to protect us from further disruption. Sometimes it's enormously tough to erect boundaries for self-preservation. Have you ever felt unbearably weighted down by the strain in your relationship, and wonder how on Earth you got to this point? Liars, cheaters, and bullies aside, sometimes we even find ourselves having to unplug from people who mean well, but really just have no clue. Next time you feel spread too thin by the demands of others, explore a few of these suggestions on how to unplug, detach, and restore your core:

- Turn off your cell phone, or silence the ringer/text and email alerts.

- Sit quietly outside.

- Don't answer the phone if it's not a good time for you to engage with that person.

- Don't respond using intelligent words to unintelligent behavior (and if you do, don't get pissed if your words go in one ear and out the other).

- Get together with friends at your home as opposed to going out.
- Instead of saying *yes* and feeling bad, just say *no* instead.
- Unplug from the dating scene for a while—don't date someone just to date.
- Turn off the TV and play a game with your kids.
- Close your office door when you have had enough office drama for the day.
- Don't check work emails when you're on vacation.
- Go to church when there is no service. Sit quietly and listen to where your thoughts take you as you embrace the silence.
- Wear flats when you feel like you should wear heels.
- Relax in a hot, salty bath.
- Put on a mood-appropriate playlist, turn it up, and tune the rest of the world out.
- Put on headphones to drown out chatter from a fellow treadmill walker or chatty airline passenger.
- Turn off the super-depressing news.
- Read a spiritually engaging book.
- Look at old photo albums (unless this will trigger feelings of resentment or hurt).
- Go to sleep early and wake up feeling armed and ready for your day.
- Watch a funny movie.

V

The letter *V* brings us three important concepts to good health: *validate, vigilant,* and *vitamins*. For starters, seek one person who will *validate* your feelings and circumstances. When you're *vigilant* you are turning over every stone for answers, you are on your toes, and you are staying as ahead of the curve as much as possible....all with eagle eyes wide open. *Vitamins* are a vital part of staying healthy but you need to do your homework before you begin taking supplements.

VALIDATE

When you feel validated, your emotions and concerns become authorized and authenticated. That is an *aha!* moment—and a very pivotal one at that. So many of us feel we have to keep our utterly dysfunctional relationship private for so many reasons. We use social media to proclaim our perfect relationship and all things "rosy" when reality is anything but. But living a lie for the benefit of others begins to erode your core. You may feel that you cannot function anymore in the warped and twisted world that you live in. Nothing makes sense, and now you even begin to doubt your own thoughts and reasoning. The resident bully can get quite angry each time you speak up or challenge things, and you may become more and more numb in order to live within the chains of a toxic relationship. That, Bella, is the point where you typically you throw out a life raft to a trusted friend or professional who will validate your feelings and situation.

My own holistic health coach validated me, and so did my friends and family. The more I heard the stupid phrases like *it takes two to make it* or *there are two sides to every coin*, the more I shut down from letting those people in. Why? Because all those sayings did was remind me that somehow, someway, I caused this. What I learned from smart women was that oftentimes *it takes two to make it and one to break it.* You had no idea you were a target. *It is not your fault.*

Who do you trust? Who is it that is wise enough to show you *how* to draw that line in the sand that says *NO MORE.* Start with one person who won't judge you, and will validate that you, as a human being, are worth and deserving of so much more.

VIGILANT

In my experience as not only a health coach, but also as woman who has loved and lost, I can say this whole process has allowed me to sharpen my vigilante skills. I don't mean that in a Clint Eastwood sort of way. I mean it in a quiet, watchful, one-step-ahead-of-the-game, hawk-eyed, observant sort of way. Bella, this toxic relationship—whether it is months long or even decades long—will chew you up and spit you out if you allow it to. Your spirit will become heavy and burdened instead of light and free. Your blood pressure will elevate along with your desire for energy from sugar, and your bodily systems will not function at capacity. Once this begins to happen, the Big Bad Wolf will see that you are becoming flustered and desperate, and he will then swoop in to be your "savior" and make everything better. This usually happens in a love language that you cannot relate to, but you have nowhere to go but "up," so you generally bite the bait.

Now is the time to recognize the cycle of abuse. When you're vigilant, during those times when you find yourself strewn into an unrecognizable pile of someone you once knew, you will not reach out for the figurative life raft from the one who pushed you overboard in the first place!

Stay vigilant about keeping your health as you become a little stronger every day. Stay aware of the manipulative cycle you are part of. Abusive relationships have a clear cycle of control that plays out time and time again. The tension phase is filled with things like insults, sarcasm, accusations, and quick mood changes. Next is the explosion stage and that involves throwing things, physical assaults, name calling, swearing, yelling, and intimidation. The last phase is the honeymoon phase when there are usually apologies, flower deliveries, gifts, promises to change, and spending time together romantically and as a family. This is where your vigilance comes in—don't get sucked into the abyss of false promises. Don't think for a minute that you are anything more than just a box to check at this point. He isn't stupid, and remember, he chose you because you are the super glue that holds your family together. He knows he can push your buttons and you will allow it because...well, you always do.

Remaining vigilant means that you stay present and watchful to all behavior. I know that people can change for the better. The key with that is that they actually have to change and keep their word. If through counseling, therapy, and open communication, the two of you can slowly enrich your relationship, then that is a dream come true. I completely understand that relationships aren't always rainbows and romance, and that even the best ones have challenging times, but when you see that you are in one that is destructive, stay vigilant. Know exactly where you are in the cycle of abuse, and reach out for help from trusted friends and professionals. Next time you get a gift that comes with an apology for horrific name calling, will you fall for it or will you say thanks but no thanks? Next time a hole gets punched in the wall in a fit of anger, will you be surprised? How will you prepare your own thoughts for the next round? *DING DING DING! In this corner, we have Bella! She is bold, beautiful, and brave, and she knows how to protect herself.*

VITAMINS

Vitamins are big business. You may feel like you need to be a guru just to know which ones to buy. I recommend that once you find a physician you trust, have blood work done so that you know where there are nutritional gaps in your diet. It is important to know what the results of your tests are. When chronic stress is a factor in your life and your immune function is at an all-time low, you may be choosing the right foods but your unhealthy gut may be keeping your body from using all those nutrients those foods provide. Taking extra supplements is not always the answer because if your gut can't digest and absorb properly, those extra vitamins won't kick it up a few notches.

Your health care provider may have some answers for you before you decide to hit the local vitamin store to self-treat symptoms. He or she can help you find out exactly what may have you feeling so exhausted. Is it a vitamin D deficiency or is it likely a love deficiency? Is it ADD (Affection Deficit Disorder) or is it low B12 that has zapped your energy, or is it working with or being married to a not-so-nice person? Many people are deficient in vitamins such as B12 and D these days. The SAD (Standard American Diet) can leave our intestinal tract sluggish and foster a landscape that doesn't promote vitamin absorption. Stress and insufficient probiotic levels in our gut greatly affect how B12 is absorbed. Vitamin D deficiencies can stem from lack of adequate sunshine, unhealthy diet, liver issues, or excess weight.

Do your homework before you spend money without knowing what to spend it on. Research vitamins and their effects. You should know what you're taking and why. Always buy the best supplements that you can afford. The best quality brands do not contain things like gluten, yeast, soy, artificial flavors, colors, fillers, or sugar, and will usually print this on the label. If you decide to buy a slew of over-the-counter vitamins, at best you are wasting money if you don't need them, and at worst you actually may be harming your health over the long term. For instance, K vitamins can counteract the effects of blood-thinning medications, and fish oils can thin the blood too much before a surgery. A little extra zinc can be very helpful to your immune system if you are around sick people a lot, like if you're a teacher or are a frequent traveler. But did you know you must take it with food or you may suffer terrible nausea? Did you know that bromelain is great for viral and bacterial sinus infections, but for best results, it must be taken with a protein-rich meal? How about that B vitamins should be taken as B complex (containing all Bs) unless your doctor says otherwise? The B vitamin family works best synergistically.

The best place to get your vitamins is always from a diet rich in whole foods—colorful, full of good fats (like avocados and nuts), fiber (vegetables and fruit), and protein (organic eggs, lean meats, and fish). If you are vegetarian then your proteins come from things like beans, nuts, seeds, tofu, and tempeh. Vegan protein powders can be a wise addition, too. A whole-person approach is the only path to true healing. What's even better is working with a super health coach who leads you...to you!

W

W is mostly about things you can do that are important to maintaining good health. Take a *walk* to catch a breath of fresh air and a good dose of sunshine or moonlight. Sometimes you need to *wait* when you're contemplating a major decision. Stay hydrated throughout the day by drinking lots of *water*. Maintain a healthy *weight* and be the best *you* you can be! Shopping at *Whole Foods Market*® can be expensive but see just what you're *not* getting for your buck. Responsible *wine* drinking is like home for me—that ever-present feeling of love and delicious memories.

WAIT

It's bizarre just how much our perception changes given the opportunity to sit and think on an issue before taking action. We have all felt the full scope of emotions from boiling over, to simmering down, to a slow warmth that can be turned down if need be. Are you that person in your marriage with the ability to call a spade and spade...you know, speak your mind? Have you cried and yelled all in an effort to become validated and heard? It is a desolate place to be in when you so desperately want to matter to someone, and nothing you do does.

Over time, with the coaching of good friends, expert counseling, and prayer, you too can learn to let things marinate before you respond. Maybe all you need is 10 minutes to cool off. Or maybe you need two weeks to ponder before you respond. But most—if not all—of the time, you will feel relief if you wait to RSVP. Father Time provides the gift of reason. The only caution is this: The more you let roll off your back, the more desensitized you can become. What do I mean? I mean that every time you sweep something under the carpet for the sake of the "whole" to avoid conflict, there is a proverbial dust pile that begins to form—under the layers of your life and well into your heart. One day, you will need to clean house from the gunk, shake it out, and toss the accumulated crap—all those unaddressed emotions. The trick here is to give yourself time to deal with issues hefty and small, but to *deal with* them eventually. Some things are ridiculously trivial and never need to be revisited again, but many aren't. Only you can decide which ones are to be put away in that figurative box, taped up, and put into storage labeled with OVER, and which ones are left out in the box labeled SO NOT OVER on the kitchen counter.

To wait—but how long? Now *that* is the question on which only you, yourself, and you can collaborate. Why don't you make the three of you a cup of tea, and ponder how long you feel you need to wait. Sit down with the mom in you, partner in you, and employee in you and see what they think.

WALK

Walking is not only incredibly slimming, but it provides an exorbitant rush of soul food for me. Some of my most gratifying walks were through the streets of Italy while sipping on a cappuccino, or on a crunchy leaf-covered trail in autumn. Maybe you, too, like to feel bundled up from head to toe to mosey through the neighborhood looking at twinkling Christmas lights. On hot summer evenings and cold winter mornings, my dear friend and I would walk briskly through the neighborhood loop and have a nice warm cup of coffee afterward. We would laugh and share so much on that walk that it felt as if it were a five-minute walk across a parking lot. Thank you Amy B. for hitting the trail with me before carpool. Our walks are so fun, I barely notice its 95 degrees…*barely!*

Brisk walking is great exercise because it's low-impact so your joints don't shout out in pain and nothing is over- or underworked. You are breathing in oxygen, the blood is circulating, and you are burning calories. Combine that with a stroll outside and you are getting a hefty dose of vitamin D, which is a vitamin (actually a hormone) that most of us are deficient in. Walking strengthens bones, too. It's crazy to imagine that our human ancestors didn't even wear shoes, yet today we wear super-soled shoes that actually can slow the bone growing process. The more impact our bones have, the more they grow and regenerate. Bones, like anything else, tend to weaken, become brittle, and deteriorate without adequate use. Thick-soled shoes, office landscapes, and our sedentary lifestyles make our bones wave the white flag, as if to say *if you don't use it, you lose it.*

So walk when you can take the elevator, walk when you could have parked closer, walk your dog, or walk with a friend. It's good for your body and good for your mind.

WATER

So many of us are walking around with our adult sippy cups these days. Bottles of water are in hand almost everywhere we go, and that's a good thing. I see fewer people with sugary drinks, and that's an even better thing! Water helps to keep our immune systems free of impurities, manage cravings, and is huge for headache sufferers.

I must mention the fact that it is critical that we all remember that Mother Earth is the provider and nurturer of all that we need, so when it comes to plastic water bottles, please recycle, refill, and reuse as often as possible. And speaking of bottled water, it is often no different than what comes out of your tap, and it seems that the really pure varieties that flow from those pristine springs down under have such a carbon footprint on them that it hardly makes one feel good about drinking them.

Then there is the BPA (*Bisphenol A*) issue. BPA, an industrial chemical that is used to make plastics, can seep into the food and beverage that is packaged in it. Even though the Food and Drug Administration (FDA) claims that it is safe, I invite you to do your own research and make your own decision. BPA exposure can cause negative health effects on the brain, endocrine system, and sex hormones. Children are at highest risk for absorbing these chemicals into their blood and tissue. For those reasons, choose a stainless steel or glass beverage container. I even take it one step further to ensure the products I use, such as my face lotion, come in glass containers.

So, back to the actual water topic: a good rule to follow is to aim for half your body weight in ounces per day. What does that look like? A woman who weighs 150 pounds should shoot for 75 ounces of water per day, or three 25-ounce bottles. Those of you who practice hot yoga or do any exercise where you sweat copious amounts, increase that amount by at least 25 percent or even more. Don't forget you're also losing important vitamins and minerals when you sweat a lot. Here's a crazy fact—things like B vitamins can turn your urine bright yellow; if you're properly hydrating, typically your urine should run clear. It's a little yucky to think about at first, but I've come to realize that in science, medicine, and prevention, the more I learn, the less shocked I become.

Many of my clients complain about water being boring and having no taste. I totally get that because although I love the hydration, curbed hunger, and mental clarity water brings, I too sometimes forget to partake. That's why I love a product called Ultima Replenisher® (which I talked about in *Hydration*) because it has no sugar or artificial sweeteners, is non-GMO and gluten-free, and is sweetened with stevia, which is all natural and doesn't spike blood sugar. It blows other sports drinks away because it tastes so good and has electrolytes, vitamins, and minerals that help replenish the salts lost during intense exercise. Can you tell I really love this stuff? Boring water no more, so no more excuses for not drinking!

I have BPA-free reusable containers that I fill up at my local Whole Foods Market® from their reverse osmosis (RO) tap for $0.39 a gallon. For as much water as I drink, there is no better value for me and my lifestyle. RO has 99 percent of the impurities taken out of it. Things like fluoride, pesticides, antibiotics, and chlorine are removed, as well as some of the necessary electrolytes. I like to add a pinch of high-quality Himalayan sea salt to my water to add back in the critical trace minerals that our bodies need. In some professional opinions, distilled water may not be the best choice for long-term hydration as it has been heated and all minerals are evaporated out. Essentially it is "dead" water and experts usually only recommend it for short-term cleanses. The main difference between RO and distilled is the process in by which the contaminants are removed. A distiller is similar to a tea kettle. The water boils, the distiller catches the steam and condenses it back into water. RO strains the water with a very tight and semi-porous membrane. Both types of water are considered very pure.

When it comes to filters, any filter is better than no filter. I think it's beyond gross that all of the antibiotics and drugs of *any* kind that are flushed down our toilet whole or passed through our digestive systems can wind up in our water supply! That image alone inspires me to make better water consumption choices, and I hope it does for you, too. Do some research on pitcher filters, carbon filters, and reverse osmosis filters. A natural spring (www.findaspring.com) is best, second is well water, and third and most popular is municipal water, which ideally should be filtered by you before you consume it.

When we live with toxic people, headaches are almost a given, so nurture yourself with more ounces of cleaner water. Mother Earth is 75 percent water and so are you! Drink in the water so you can improve your health and get your beautiful self out into the world.

WEIGHT

As a woman in America, I find it terribly disturbing how much attention is put not only on our weight, but also the size of our pants, bras, and shoes. These numbers seem to have the ability to define us over traits like kindness, loyalty, and respect. I think young girls today have it even tougher than we did, and that's just ridiculous. For every positive advertising campaign, like the Dove real beauty message about loving your body or ads depicting full-figured models, we see even more messages touting the exact opposite—that thin is sexy. The truth of the matter is it's quite difficult to find the beauty within ourselves— regardless of what we weigh—when all around us, all day, every day, is the message is that *THIN IS SEXY*. We can throw blame at advertisers, Barbie dolls, pop stars, or men, but until we see ourselves as beautiful and healthy, that message will ring loud and often for our daughters unless we teach them—and ourselves—to tune them out.

So how do you tune it out? Let's twist it around: instead of *THIN IS SEXY*, change the message to *NO MATTER WHAT YOU WEIGH, YOU'RE BEING THE BEST VERSION OF YOU THAT YOU COULD POSSIBLY BE.* You *are* beautiful. Do you feel that way? Take this opportunity to strengthen not your abs or your glutes, but your faith. Stick with me here -

Max Lucado, the Christian children's book author, tells the story of Punchinello, the little wooden carved boy who lives in a world where he feels compelled to go along with what the masses deem cool or worthy. Yet he has a void that cannot be filled by the latest gizmo or gadget. He is called to connect to his maker and is reminded that God doesn't make mistakes. He is perfect just the way he is. Hmmmm…sounds familiar, doesn't it?

You see, we are all built differently, have different genes, and have vastly different lifestyles. We humans come in all shapes and sizes. In order to see yourself as beautiful, you have to toss the mainstream ideas of what beauty is and embrace how your maker made you, and then work at being the best version of you. That's how we honor ourselves and honor God. Do you feel like those extra 15 pounds are preventing you from that goal?

The bottom line (pun intended) to good health is attaining a healthy weight. It is imperative to your physical and mental well-being and to the aging process. Excessive weight affects your insulin production, thyroid function, testosterone (sex drive for men and women), estrogen, stress hormones, melatonin, belly fat, headaches, and inflammation in the ankles, knees, and back…the list goes on. "Waist" management is crucial to cleaning up your life, and allowing your body to reset in order to be able to thrive. Be the best version of you by maintaining a healthy weight.

WHOLE FOODS MARKET®

I'm beyond lucky because the area where I live is home to four Whole Foods Markets®. Unfortunately, Whole Foods Market® also seems to go by the names Whole Budget or Whole Paycheck. Let's touch on that for a moment here. The truth is yes, many items seem expensive, but many products cost more because of how they are made, stored, and the ingredients they contain.

Take almond butter, for example. Raw, organic almond butter sells for $15.99 a jar at Whole Foods Market®, and a mainstream brand of almond butter sells for $4.99 a jar at Walmart® or Target®. Seems like a no-brainer, doesn't it? Let's look a little closer…

Raw nuts (raw foods in general) contain more essential nutrients and enzymes because they haven't been destroyed by heat like their roasted brethren. When you buy organic, you're really paying for what you *don't* get: even though almonds have shells, in mainstream farming, the entire plant is doused in pesticides, herbicides, and fungicides. So, the cheaper jar will get you a heaping teaspoon of nutrient deficient nuts, pesticides, and most likely some hydrogenated oils and added sugars, all for the low bargain price of $4.99. The organic jar contains a food grown without chemicals, and maximizes nutrient content while reducing toxicity levels. This absolutely costs more money from the seed-to-shelf process. I always recommend the splurge on organics whenever possible. Compare *exact brand* prices at different stores because wasting money isn't living with gusto!

Reading ingredient lists are always so important, as is knowing that the best quality brands aren't always packaged in the coolest and shiniest packages. All that means is that the company has a big advertising budget, not necessarily the best product. What is for certain is that buying non-GMO (genetically modified organism), organic, local, toxin-free foods and body care products *do* cost more.

However, that brings us back to the investment in the fortification and well-being of you, and protecting and honoring your health as much as possible. Do you want to pay now, or pay later? Think of it as health insurance...a little extra now goes a long way later when you really need it to.

You don't need a savvy shopper degree in order to maximize your experience in a store like Whole Foods Market®. You just need a little patience—and maybe a good health coach (www.jeaninefinelli.com)!

WINE

By now, I'm sure you know that vino is an enjoyable part of my life. Not because I overindulge or spend too much money on it, but because it's a big association with *home* for me. Ever since I can remember, wine was on the table around which my loved ones convened. We shared stories over wine, ate scrumptious meals alongside it, and laughed, sang, and cried into it. Wine embodies the emotions of my life, and growing up in an Italian family in the Bronx, it is to my table setting as Vatican City is to Italy.

My mom tells a story of when I was about four years old and I thought it would be a yummy and exciting idea to finish the wine that was left in everyone's glass after a large family dinner with many guests. Wine was so much a part of the meal like the crusty Italian bread and the olives we put on our fingers, that I had no idea it would make me feel awful after a few too many sips! There is so much childlike innocence in that for me! How amazing that even after that little experience, I grew up seeing red wine as necessary as a fork and spoon. Once my sisters and I got older, we were allowed to have a sip with Sunday dinner or on holidays. I say *sip* because our portions were always watered down by a ratio of 15 parts Coke to one part wine, not to mention the ice cubes. Nonetheless, we felt so grown up and beyond our tender years with our "adult" beverages.

Over the years, I've refined my palate in a nice wine snob sort of way. I do feel that anyone who enjoys the svelteness of a rare vintage—no matter who they are or where they live—would have the same thing happen to their taste buds. It's simple, really—once you've had better you want better and I believe that goes for anything—wine, men, friends, joy, jobs. If you enjoy wine and want to learn more about it, make friends at your local wine shop and learn more about the wines you like and try new ones. Join their email list and find out when they are offering special deals. I have become a savvy shopper in the grape department, and while I still become joyous when opening a noble bottle to share with friends, I am equally as joyous to open a $10 bottle and have a glass while writing this book on a Saturday night.

I have learned that everything has a price tag in life. Everything. The $90 bottle tasted heavenly but was accompanied by the words and negativity of the person who was pouring it, which made it into liquid poison for me. The cheaper bottle and better company has the power to make me feel like a million bucks.

Do you enjoy wine? Have you treated yourself to a better bottle lately? What grape do you prefer and why? Studies say that a glass a day is beneficial, while anything more than that has the opposite effect. Don't forget that alcohol can be one of the biggest thieves of sleep. When life calls for gusto, share some vino with those you *amore*!

X

I've taken a few liberties with X, so stick with me here! When you X *foliate*, you lend a helping hand to your lymphatic system. And when you X *out*—just like closing Windows—you're giving yourself permission to take a little break from what's challenging you at the moment.

X FOLIATE

The process of detox is all encompassing, right? When you are ridding your body of stored toxins from nutritional and emotional slaughter, a great way to speed up that process is dry skin brushing. It exfoliates that skin and sloughs off dead cells all while clearing out toxins below the skin. I confess the first time I heard about this technique I wasn't running out to buy a skin brush. But one day I picked up an all-natural bristle skin brush, and I researched online about how to skin brush. Most sites said the same thing: begin with long slow strokes starting at your toes and feet, and work up to your knees, then knees to hip, hip over buttocks, buttocks to abdomen, abdomen to heart. Next you go fingers to elbow, elbow to shoulders, shoulders to heart. Some websites recommended staying away from your breasts, others said just go very gently there. Dry skin brushing feels really good and makes your skin feel tingly. The pressure you apply shouldn't hurt, but you do want to get some feeling into it.

The point is when you exfoliate by skin brushing, you are moving toxins that are stored in your lymphatic system toward your heart so it can better circulate for elimination by using the bathroom or sweating. The lymphatic system is sometimes regarded as the quieter sister of the circulatory system, but is crucial to the body's ability to defend against all sorts of issues from cellulite to cancer. Unfortunately, it seems that many western physicians don't understand the importance of the lymphatic system and, therefore, their patients are in the dark as well. When an infection causes swollen glands or swollen lymph nodes, there is likely an underlying illness that hopefully can be treated properly. The fluid in your lymphatic system clears away toxins from your cells and is powered only by breathing and movement. Think of a bathtub with a broken drain filled with dirty water. You don't want that in your body! Yuck! Now is a great time to remind you that getting regular professional massages helps to detox and lower stress!

Lymphatic massage, exercise, and exfoliation are three of the best ways to clear out the "dirty tub of water" that lies underneath your skin. The whole process should take about five minutes while standing in the shower before you turn it on...that's why it's called *dry* skin brushing. This whole process exfoliates the skin on your entire body, which is often overlooked unless you're slathering it with low-quality, artificial "moisturizers." Regular lymphatic dry brushing and massages will also take much of the detox burden off of your kidneys and liver. Want to have the skin of a baby's bum and glow a little more? Get yourself a dry skin brush with a long handle and natural fibers. Retailers everywhere sell them. Our ancestors have been doing this for centuries, so love yourself to health from the inside out, Bella.

X OUT

We all know how to "X out" of open windows while working on the computer. One day when my daughter was about seven years old, we were outside jumping on the trampoline, and she said she was going to "just X out" for a rest. The simple fact of being able to X out of something other than a document really intrigued me. From the mouths of babes comes unexpected wisdom. I needed that lesson and the ability to give myself a free pass. Why *can't* we just X out of things when we need a break? This goes hand-in-hand with learning to say *no*, and it can mean that perhaps you will want to revisit things another time, but that time is just not now.

Look at "Xing" out as a disengaging mechanism that preserves energy or mental peace even if just for a few moments. Here are some "xamples" of what you can X out of:

- A yoga flow that is just too much for your body that day. X out and lie on your mat – rejoin in for the next flow.

- Facebook friend requests where the intention isn't mutual.

- Answering that call if you are too pressed for time.

- Ordering another Cosmo even if everyone else at the table is whooping it up.

- Sitting on the couch when you can go for a walk outside instead.

- Stooping down to the fish-food level behavior of others. You're not a bottom feeder, Bella!

So, what are you going to X out of today? Don't judge yourself for being human. Maybe you will re-open that "application," and maybe you won't. Either way, the choice is yours and yours alone. It's all part of living your own "dash"—that dash between the year you were born and the year you die. Choose you.

Y

Y is about practice. Practice saying *yes* to a life that brings you happiness and inner fulfillment. Practice envisioning where you want to be a *year* from now. Practice *yoga* to challenge yourself physically and to get in touch with who you really are.

YEAR

A year from now probably seems like light years away. Am I right? Your brain is brimming with so many thoughts and questions. Work deadlines and trips fill up your calendar along with home improvements or moving dates, classroom donations and volunteering, teacher gifts, doctor appointments, haircuts, court dates, school functions, lawyer appointments, vacations, and so many other accountabilities. Do you remember being a child and how long the weeks were leading up to your birthday? Time sure flies faster and faster with every passing year, doesn't it? Today is the day to do something that your future self will thank you for because one year from today will be here before you know it.

Make the most of your days—even the ones that knock you down and leave you feeling powerless. They will pass, but how you manage to get through them is partly up to you. Where do you want to be one year from now? Do you want to have peace? Do you want to lose weight? Do you want to be in a loving relationship? Do you want a new career? Ask yourself what it is that you want and begin today to do one thing to get you closer to that goal. One thing that is for sure is this—you don't want to be where you are in one year, so start making some changes that really matter! Get ready to celebrate on New

Year's Eve—or heck, even tonight—and toast to your *You Year Resolution*. Grab life with both hands—gusto required!

YES

Now that you are beginning to say *no* to accepting the supporting actress role in someone else's charade, you will need to practice saying *yes* a whole lot more. Yes, you deserve respect. Yes, it's okay to crave love and intimacy. Yes, this toxic relationship is so over!

Remember to find comfort in the fact that a relationship can never strengthen when both people are not committed to just that. If you have both feet in, and your partner has two feet and nine toes out, then yes, it is time for a super-sized change. Today is a good day to find your inner child and ask her what she thinks. She is in there, inside of you. Does she deserve the life she is living…a life unlived, unhappy, and unfulfilled? If your answer is *no*, then say *yes* to living a life filled with vibrancy.

Remember, you are the lotus flower whose flamboyant petals are covered up with dirt, but that is exactly how it is supposed to be at this point, and there is no way around it. Just like that little flower, keep reaching up and saying *yes, yes, yes!* to the warmth of the sunlight. With every yes comes lucidity. It awaits your arrival. There is no way around it, only through it, Bella.

YOGA

You're probably clued in by now…I fell in love with yoga. Truly. It led me to me, and I loved what I found. I found a woman who was a tightly wound ball of nerves, but sought freedom. I found a woman who had allowed the restriction in her heart to become restriction in her abs. I found a woman who felt broken and yet desperately craved a life that made her feel whole. My yoga practice did this for me as it connected my breath to my body, my heart to my mind, and my spirit to God.

Yoga isn't just about being "bendy." The practice is about carving out time to love yourself—your entire self. It's about honoring the parts of your body that ache and softening your movements for the most delicate parts of you. It's about challenging those areas that you feel can handle more intensity. It's about letting go of everything you think you should be and feel "at your age," and it's about not only glistening with sweat on the outside but reveling in the moment when you feel your inner child smile on the inside.

Do you have to constantly "play nice with others" throughout your day? Do you have to bite your tongue, hold your breath, and put your needs last in order to meet everyone else's? We all do, but no more! Yoga is the only place where I can put my mat down and completely check out of whatever is going on in my life outside of the studio. It is the small piece of real estate, my mat, where the most growth happens for me as I honor what I have done, what I cannot do, and what I would like to do.

I implore you to find a local studio and try a class. Every class is different and so are the teachers. You will find your favorite teachers along the way for various reasons, but each teacher will challenge you in a different way. Some teachers test your ability to be still and breathe through restlessness while others will challenge you to hold a pose longer and deeper than you ever though humanly possible. Don't worry, you won't be the only one saying a few expletives in your mind while you wait to hear the word *release*! Find out what is simmering inside of you and let it out. You may even find yourself emotional during class and wonder to yourself, *what on Earth is happening here?* Don't' worry about trying to figure it out, just roll with it.

Your inner child comes out to play during yoga and she can kick your butt if you don't recognize her and become her. She only wants 60 to 90 minutes of your time. Experiment with regular yoga and hot yoga, different teachers, and different classes. Yoga supports bodily functions, bone health, and stress and weight management. During a 90-minute hot yoga class, an adult woman can burn between 700 to 1,000 calories! I thought that would get your attention! So get to work finding a studio. Just promise me one thing first—no guilt about what you *should* be doing instead. Unless you have strict orders from a doctor, you *should* be doing yoga.

Thank you Amy F. for encouraging me to go with you to my first class! Thank you Tina V., my friend and very first teacher. You didn't make me feel like a complete loser when I showed up for a level two class barely knowing what Downward Facing Dog was. I love you, my amazing friends.

Z

So here we find ourselves at *Z*, the last stop on the train to good health! *(Destination) Zero* isn't really a place, it's a state of mind, a state of contentment. The Bible says there's a time to laugh and a time to cry. I'd like to add that there's also a time to *zip it*. When you do, you're taking back the power you so richly deserve.

ZIP IT

There were countless times when I would engage rationally with an irrational person. Fat lot of good it did, too. I know you know exactly what I'm talking about. How frustrating is it when you continually argue your point and come up empty? Regardless of what you say, it will never make a difference in how he reacts to you. What happens is that the more you talk, the more they talk back with words that injure your heart, hence continuing the cycle of you feeling defeated and frustrated. So spare yourself the agony and just zip it.

When you zip it, you actually take back your control and unplug from allowing more toxicity in—not to mention lowering your blood pressure. Maybe your lesson here is to let things marinate—not in the hope of effective further communication, just in the hope that you can look within yourself and find what *your* lesson in this mess is. Next time you find yourself in the crazy and maniacal loop of one of these pointless debates, zip it. Someone can't engage with you, control you, and get you all revved up if you take back your energy! They cannot play tug-of-war alone.

So just zip it for now. Grab your purse and head out for the day, or take the kids for ice cream or to grandma's house. While you think you may be helping yourself by talking or defending yourself, you really aren't. The time will come for you to be heard, but now is not that time. You know you are factual and make sense, so find peace in that. Don't worry what your toxic partner thinks. Rarely does he think of you and your feelings…and you most likely aren't being thought of now. So, what are you going to do with a few free hours today? Choose to step away from the three-ring circus and get on with *your* day *your* way.

(DESTINATION) ZERO

Destination Zero is a term that my best friend shared with me one day. It's not really a place. It is the concept that at that exact moment in time, there is zero experience of craving, wanting, longing, missing, or needing. It is such a sacred little spot where all senses are aligned and there is zero lack. You know you're there when you are filled with peace, contentment, and assuredness. How does it happen? I'm not entirely sure, but I think it is a collaboration among Lady Luck, making benevolent decisions, living authentically, and getting a wink from God letting you know you are on to something that you should keep doing. That intensely sweet feeling that arriving at Destination Zero brings is quite possibly a reward for nothing more than opening your heart to God's plan for you.

PEACE, BLISS, ADVENTURE... THIS WAY!

Life is a crazy journey, not a destination. No one knows that more than you. Thank you, Bella, for letting me share my journey with you as you walk through yours. I truly hope my story and the things that helped me through my trying times have helped you heal and become whole.

As you tiptoe through this three-ring circus of life, you must make loving yourself a priority. My hope is that the ABCs in this book have shown you that you absolutely do have the power to rewrite the ending of your own story. Although it is no simple task, the power is ultimately yours when choosing how to react to sources of stress in your life. You have the power to choose what you eat and what you drink. You have the power to create better sleep habits, and you have the power to surround yourself with people who encompass wholeness and vitality. Most importantly, you have the power to say *yes* to wanting more out of this beautiful life. Despite all of the roadblocks ahead, you have the power to stand up for what is true and real, and by doing just that, you will become a living, breathing example of how to Love Yourself to Health to those around you. Whether your "go to" for joy is a Latitude Adjustment, Music, or an Aloe-Tini, it's time to live like you mean it and Love Yourself to Health.

That intense, immobilized-with-fear feeling that prevents you from seeing a glorious future will shift just when you least expect it. One day...*POUF!* There it is. Expect to feel a breath of life grow within you—not unlike that same process when the caterpillar begins to grow colorful wings while in the darkest and most confined moment of its tiny life. You, too, will experience a complete metamorphosis from who you once were to who you are meant to be, only guided by the hands of Divine Love.

169

You may hear yourself saying, "Never again!" But never say never, Bella, because more love might just come your way like never before. True *amore* is two people wanting to give one another exactly what they crave in return: honesty, respect, and super amounts of fun! Life is for living. Your future is like a little gondola built for two…it's waiting for you on the shores of your own Venetian waterway. It will wait forever and be there when you are ready, although it quietly calls to you, *sooner rather than later*. It belongs only to you. It will sit patiently, rhythmically rocking, and wait for the day when you walk down to the water's edge and step in with both feet. From there you will set adrift on new horizons in your life, quite possibly with one hand being lovingly held, and maybe a glass of wine in the other.

Now, go out there, Bella, and grab your life by the calzones or someone else will. And remember…

L'amore è amore paziente è gentile. Love is patient, love is kind.

CPSIA information can be obtained
at www.ICGtesting.com
Printed in the USA
FFOW05n0554250914

9 781771 431699